CultureShock!
A Survival Guide to Customs and Etiquette

Marie Louise Graff

Marshall Cavendish
Editions

This edition published in 2008 by:
Marshall Cavendish Corporation
99 White Plains Road
Tarrytown, NY 10591-9001
www.marshallcavendish.us

Other Marshall Cavendish Offices:
Marshall Cavendish International (Asia) Private Limited. 1 New Industrial Road,
Singapore 536196 ∎ Marshall Cavendish Ltd. 5th Floor, 32–38 Saffron Hill,
London EC1N 8FH, UK ∎ Marshall Cavendish International (Thailand) Co Ltd.
253 Asoke, 12th Flr, Sukhumvit 21 Road, Klongtoey Nua, Wattana, Bangkok
10110, Thailand ∎ Marshall Cavendish (Malaysia) Sdn Bhd, Times Subang,
Lot 46, Subang Hi-Tech Industrial Park, Batu Tiga, 40000 Shah Alam, Selangor
Darul Ehsan, Malaysia

Marshall Cavendish is a trademark of Times Publishing Limited

ISBN 10: 0-7614-5496-9
ISBN 13: 978-0-7614-5496-0

Please contact the publisher for the Library of Congress catalog number

Printed in China by Everbest Printing Co Ltd

Photo Credits:
All black and white photos by or from the author except pages x, 3, 8, 11, 13,
62, 64, 113, 120, 125, 138, 165, 201, 220–221 (Alex Drummond); pages 22,
162, 171 (Larry Horner); pages 58, 69, 141, 145, 192, 203 (Louise Horner);
pages 12, 77, 150, 180, 185 (Jill Richards) and pages 85, 159 (Amy Sholtz).
Colour photos from: Getty Images pages a, b–c, e, n (top); Photolibrary pages
d, f–g, h, i, j–k, l–m, n (bottom), o, p. ∎ Cover photo: Lonely Planet Images

All illustrations by TRIGG

ABOUT THE SERIES

Culture shock is a state of disorientation that can come over anyone who has been thrust into unknown surroundings, away from one's comfort zone. *CultureShock!* is a series of trusted and reputed guides which has, for decades, been helping expatriates and long-term visitors to cushion the impact of culture shock whenever they move to a new country.

Written by people who have lived in the country and experienced culture shock themselves, the authors share all the information necessary for anyone to cope with these feelings of disorientation more effectively. The guides are written in a style that is easy to read and covers a range of topics that will arm readers with enough advice, hints and tips to make their lives as normal as possible again.

Each book is structured in the same manner. It begins with the first impressions that visitors will have of that city or country. To understand a culture, one must first understand the people—where they came from, who they are, the values and traditions they live by, as well as their customs and etiquette. This is covered in the first half of the book.

Then on with the practical aspects—how to settle in with the greatest of ease. Authors walk readers through how to find accommodation, get the utilities and telecommunications up and running, enrol the children in school and keep in the pink of health. But that's not all. Once the essentials are out of the way, venture out and try the food, enjoy more of the culture and travel to other areas. Then be immersed in the language of the country before discovering more about the business side of things.

To round off, snippets of basic information are offered before readers are 'tested' on customs and etiquette of the country. Useful words and phrases, a comprehensive resource guide and list of books for further research are also included for easy reference.

CONTENTS

FOREWORD

Spain is a land of contrasts. A fascinating mixture of cultures, architecture, landscapes and climates, it is a country begging to be explored and offering newcomers as wide a choice of lifestyles, business opportunities and entertainment as any other country in Europe.

Spain's history is equally contrasting. One of the most ancient countries in Europe, it has survived numerous conquests, religious wars and violent upheavals. From being one of the wealthiest and most powerful countries in the world during the reign of the Catholic Kings, through a devastating civil war from which it took the country many years to recover, to today, when Spain is considered one of the more progressive countries in Europe with a stable economy and a choice of climates to suit even the most demanding tastes.

Although Spain is a fast changing country, many people, particularly in the countryside, go about their daily life in a traditional way. This farmer prefers a leisurely form of transport to modern, motorised vehicles.

So many people have been so very helpful that to try and list everyone by name would fill the book before it got started.

Writing this book proved to be a fascinating experience! However well you may think you know the country you live in, you find you learn a surprising amount of new 'facts' when it comes to writing a book about it. However, any attempts at generalising about the culture of a country must begin with a disclaimer... no matter how much research may have gone into it, the result cannot avoid being coloured by the views and attitudes of the author.

My husband and I visited Spain originally in 1953 and have been living on the Costa Blanca, off and on, since 1973. All five members of our family agree that choosing to retire in Spain was perhaps the best thing we ever did. Without determined encouragement from my daughter Josie, I wouldn't have dared tackle the project but she kept insisting "You can do it, Ma!" and jollied me along when I wavered. My grateful thanks for her perseverance.

MAP OF SPAIN

BAY OF BISCAY

FRANCE

BALEARIC SEA

SPAIN

PORTUGAL

●
MADRID

BALEARIC ISLANDS

MEDITERRANEAN
SEA

NORTH
ATLANTIC
OCEAN

ALGERIA

MOROCCO

FIRST IMPRESSIONS

'I would rather be first in a little
Iberian village than second in Rome.'
—Julius Caesar

ANY FOREIGNER LIVING IN SPAIN will, to a certain degree, always remain a foreigner. You may have adapted beautifully to living in Spain, yet the Spanish culture will always remain different. This difference stems from the history of the country, the background to all the people who are 'Spanish' and 'Spaniards'. A foreigner may become Spanish by nationality, may even think and act like a Spaniard, but will never be a Spaniard at heart.

If you make little or no attempt to understand this history, you will remain just another foreigner living in Spain and will have little patience with the 'differences' you may encounter. If you make the effort to read a little about the country and its people and learn some Spanish, your experience in Spain will be enriched, and any possible culture shock may not be so traumatic.

If you are observant, you will soon learn to interpret the behaviour of a Spaniard, and as a consequence know how you should behave yourself. Manners are extremely important. Spaniards, although proud, are by nature polite and courteous. They are usually kind to foreigners. You do not need to imitate *how* a Spaniard eats to be accepted, but it is advisable to eat *when* he does. Demanding an evening meal at six o'clock may encounter resistance, and you should not expect Spaniards to accept an invitation if you insist on keeping to meal times with which they are unfamiliar.

A GOOD FIRST IMPRESSION

My impression of the Spain which existed when we paid our first visit in 1959 was "How delightful!". Spaniards seemed such friendly, courteous people who didn't seem in any way prepared to take advantage of us 'ignorant foreigners' but more disposed to offer as much help and advice as possible to make us feel welcome. We had driven from Naples along the Mediterranean coast through the South of France and into northern Spain and my husband and I agreed that Spaniards generally seemed extremely relaxed, dignified and honest people. We had been told to watch out for the Guardia Civil who had a reputation for being tough but in fact we found them to be extremely 'civil' and quite prepared to go out of their way to be helpful. In fact, in later years, they have always proved to be just that.

'Moon Country'

I have to confess the our first impression of the Spanish landscape was that it was 'moon country', simply because we were used to the lush, tropical vegetation of Singapore and Malaysia.

Spain had been suffering drought conditions and was very brown and dusty that first summer and the mountain areas we drove through seemed stark and bare. Once we settled here and witnessed changes in the rainfall and got used to the surroundings, we found ourselves getting fonder and fonder of many things: the mountains, particularly in spring when they abound in wild flowers; the almond blossom blanketing the terraces; the very terraces themselves, all neatly ranged up and down mountain sides; the sweet-smelling orange orchards and the vineyards which turn gold and red and brown in the autumn. In fact, we suddenly realised that we really loved the landscape we had at one time considered to be 'moon country'. As we became more familiar with Spain as a whole rather than just our immediate surroundings, it was clear that the country could offer just about any type of landscape anyone might wish for with the added bonus of one of the best climates in the world.

A Christmas Rescue

One Christmas, we decided to go up into the mountains for a picnic. My granddaughter Lara was only two years old at the time and we always took her pushchair with us because she could only walk short distances under her own steam and was already too heavy to be carried far. We decided to explore a new area and found a lovely country road winding away from the main road into terraced areas. Here we eventually found a shady spot off the road. A deep ditch ran between us and our chosen spot but a narrow, cement bridge appeared to be sturdy enough to take the weight of the car so, without further ado, I turned the vehicle and was halfway across when one of the tyres slid off the bridge and we crunched to a halt.

At first we thought we could hoist the car up ourselves by finding logs and rocks to put under the wheel but after several efforts, which only seemed to make matters worse, we realised that we would have to find help. My son-in-law was dispatched with Lara in her pushchair to the main road to stop whatever traffic might come by and ask for assistance but it was getting late and cars on those roads were usually few and far between.

It was therefore a tremendous relief when, about twenty minutes later, we saw a Guardia Civil van approaching. The two officers had folded up the pushchair and put Lara and her father into the back of their van to bring them back to us. They then wasted no time. My car was back on the road after only a few minutes! Lara still remembers her exciting ride in the Guardia Civil van!

MAKING AN EFFORT

'When in Spain, do as the Spaniards do' should be your motto—within the boundaries of common sense, of course. No need to abandon your own standards and culture in order to become Spanish. You are an *extranjero* (foreigner) and will remain an *extranjero*, but 'correct behaviour' will be appreciated and, if it does not earn you total acceptance, it will at least ensure that you receive cooperative friendliness.

Some expatriates arrive, settle down and remain. Others arrive, cannot settle and go away, taking all their grievances and prejudices with them. They are usually those who make no effort to understand the Spanish mentality but try to impose their own standards of behaviour on the people they encounter. Instead of trying to rush things, they should learn to relax. Spaniards tend to concentrate on enjoying the 'here and now' and letting 'tomorrow' take care of itself.

TOURISM

Your first impression of Spain may be one of tourism. Tourism has changed the face of Spain forever. Small fishing towns have expanded into cosmopolitan centres with large tourist hotels, marinas, skyscrapers and sprawling housing developments. Spain tends to become 'tourist' Spain, with 'pop' *flamenco*, second-rate bullfights and mass-produced souvenirs. The tourist can survive without having to eat Spanish food, drink Spanish wine, read Spanish newspapers, or even try to speak Spanish.

Yet travel only a few kilometres inland and you will discover villages, towns, even cities, hardly touched by the coastal transformation. Unlike many places on the coast, they retain much of their traditional way of life, dignity and values and an admirable degree of cultural integrity, with each place maintaining its own individuality. Much of Spain is in fact like this.

In Spanish towns and villages untouched by tourism, the relationship between people and the land is a very close one. Agriculture is still very important: women work in the local fruit and vegetable packing factories, and most families grow crops. Family life is paramount. The tradition for the parents to provide homes for sons when they marry means that many of the original small houses have been extended upwards or outwards to fulfil this commitment.

THE LAND AND ITS HISTORY

CHAPTER 2

'The earth belongs to the living, not to the dead.'
—Thomas Jefferson

ONE OF THE FIRST CONSIDERATIONS when deciding where to settle in Spain is what sort of climate you are looking for. Spain offers you a wide range to choose from. Basically a land of brilliant hot sunshine and cold black shade, Spanish landscapes and climates are anything but monotonous.

Spain, the third largest nation in Europe, occupies most of the Iberian peninsula. It covers a total area of 504,782 sq km (194,897 miles) including the Balearic islands in the Mediterranean sea, the Canary islands off the western coast of Africa as well as Ceuta and Melilla, free ports on the northern coast of Africa and several other small islands off the coast of Morocco.

DIVERSE CLIMATES
The Far North, also known as Green Spain
Galicia, in the north-west, is often likened to West Ireland, with plentiful rainfall producing lush green hillsides and half-submerged valleys called *rias*. Further along the coast, Asturias with its wild countryside and coal mines is more like South Wales. The pastoral farming and sound of cow bells in Cantabria next door could almost make you believe you were in Switzerland. The Basque country also presents an alpine aspect with farmhouses like Swiss chalets. During winter it rains almost continuously, producing vegetation of an intense shade of green not to be found elsewhere in the country. The Pyrenees foothills are like the Scottish

Highlands, but if you go further south into Navarre, you will find vast stretches of tawny-golden undulating countryside around Pamplona and vast expanses of vineyards as you go even further south. Central Spain includes the provinces of La Rioja, Castile-Leon, Castile-La Mancha, Extremadura and the capital Madrid. This region is characterised by its elevated plateaus and arid climate. The Sierra de Guadarrama and Sierra de Gredos to the north and west of Madrid provide perfect winter playgrounds. North-east of Madrid, La Rioja is famous for its extensive vineyards. To the south, the land is harsh and sunbaked. This whole region is located on a vast plateau, the Meseta.

The Meseta

It may surprise a newcomer to discover that Spain, one of the largest and hottest countries in Europe, is also one of the highest. Apart from the Ebro and Guadalquivir valleys, the coastal plains rise sharply up to the Meseta, the vast central plateau which is approximately 600 m (2,000 ft) high and covers two-fifths of the peninsula. Here, the bright light can hurt your eyes and temperatures soar in summer and plummet in winter. You can travel for miles and miles and never see a person or a village.

TRIGG

The Castilian countryside is a stony landscape and boulders litter the fields surrounding Avila and Segovia. The soil is poor, as it is in Extremadura, a wild remote region that provides a glimpse into an older Spain.

Mediterranean Spain

In the shadow of the north-eastern Pyrenees, Catalonia´s landscape changes from cold valleys and rugged coastlines to fertile *huertas*, coastal and irrigated plains rich with citrus orchards. Valencia, further south, is home to citrus orchards, date palms and fig trees, as well as almond orchards, olive groves and extensive vineyards. Murcia, even further south, is the driest part but its irrigated hillsides, however, are dotted with fertile *huertas* known for yielding excellent produce.

The countryside becomes drier and more mountainous the further south you go until you reach the desert/moon landscape around Almeria which was featured in spaghetti Westerns of the 1960s.

The balmy climate all over Spain allows you to have a drink at an outdoor café even in winter.

Southern Spain

Andalusia comes closest to most foreigners' idea of Spain, perhaps because tourist promotion posters usually show a bullfighter in his fancy regalia, or a beautiful *señorita* in her spotted *flamenco* dress strumming a guitar. Such images are more readily found in the south.

The landscape here is varied and powerful. The snow-capped Sierra Nevada range contains Spain's highest peaks. The great river Guadalquivir is surrounded by fertile pastures, marshlands and beaches. Stud farms and bull ranches abound. Here, too, is brilliant sunshine and deep shadows.

The Muslims from North Africa occupied this area for nearly 800 years and left a deep impression, especially in its architecture. Buildings are whitewashed to keep them cool and, in the bright sunlight, the effect is simply dazzling.

Villages nestling on a hillside are a common sight in Spain. Conditions may be more primitive, but living in a village is a wonderful experience.

Great builders of infrastructure, the Romans left behind many vestiges of their stay in Spain: aqueducts, fortifications, amphitheatres, etc. dot the Spanish countryside. Some aqueducts are still in working condition today.

The Rain in Spain

Parts of Spain which are on the arid side may only have as little as 203 mm (8 inches) of rain a year but those 8 inches may all fall in a single day. On the Costa Blanca, this type of rainfall usually occurs towards the end of summer, and the first really big storm, accompanied by thunder and lightning and torrential rains, is called the *gota fria* (cold drop). Havoc quite often results because streets do not have drains or gutters and torrents of water will cascade down towards the sea, sweeping away everything lying in their path. Flash floods can occur with surprising ease and cause serious damage.

Sahara Rain

You might be surprised one day to be caught in a rain shower and come home with either you or your car covered in muddy splashes. This does not mean that you carelessly drove through muddy pools; it means that the rainfall contained a fair portion of Sahara sand which, being pinkish in colour, stains everything it lands on, including your recently painted brilliant white villa and the tiles in your freshly cleaned pool. Your garden too, will look as if it is suffering from some strange leprous disease. You may have to hire a high-pressure hose to remove the stains but you will be glad to know that this will not need to be done more than once or twice a year.

The island of Gomera boasts of a rare species of *oleander*. This variety of green shrub with its fragrant white or purple flowers is considered a 'living fossil', a remnant of a past geological age.

A CHEQUERED HISTORY

One of the largest countries in Europe, Spain offers not only a wide variety of climates and landscapes but also a fascinating mixture of people with different cultural backgrounds. No one area nor any one Spaniard can be said to be 'typically Spanish'.

In order to understand and appreciate Spain and its complexities, you need to know a bit about the upheavals that the country has suffered throughout history.

Early Times

Little is known of the original inhabitants of the Iberian peninsula. They were, however, responsible for one of the most famous examples of cave paintings in the world, the 'Sistine Chapel of the Neolithic Age' at Altamira. By around 2000 BC, the Phoenicians, then the Greeks, established trading colonies on Spain's Mediterranean shores. They came in search of silver, lead, copper and tin, and founded flourishing trading counters.

The Roman Invasion

After the Greeks came the Romans who became masters of all Iberia during the 1st century BC. By the second half of the 3rd century, they had founded sizeable Christian communities whose social, cultural and juridical structures were well developed. The Iberian colonies thrived in the Roman Empire, producing three Roman emperors and several distinguished literary figures such as the Senecas, Martial and Lucan. The Roman influence is evident in the Romance languages spoken by the people: Castilian, Catalan and Gallego are all derived from Latin. The Romans have also left some outstanding physical evidence of their presence. Segovia's aqueduct and the theatre and other ruins at Merida in Extremadura are imposing examples of Roman architectural achievements.

Historical Cities

According to an ancient legend, Seville was actually founded by Hercules whilst on his adventures. The ancient city of Cadiz, also in Andalusia, is located on the Atlantic coast and proudly claims to be the oldest continuously inhabited city in the Western world.

The Germans

Germanic invaders swept through Europe in the early part of the 5th century and overran the Roman settlements. The Visigoths established the first unified kingdom about a hundred years later. However, the leaders adopted a Roman style of government and converted to the Catholic faith. Thus the Roman civilisation survived three centuries of Germanic rule until the arrival of the Moors.

THE MIDDLE AGES

Arab invasions from northern Africa in AD 711 produced a new society which combined three distinct ethnic and religious groups. Christians and Jews, who had lived side by side for several centuries, were now joined by Muslims. Their mutual tolerance and collaboration led to an extremely rich culture resulting in such architectural masterpieces as the Grand Mosque in Cordoba, the Giralda in Seville and the Alhambra in Granada.

A Natural Wonder

The Alhambra in Granada is probably one of the few 'wonders of the world' in which you might want to live. The Generalife with its famous gardens, is less well kept but its atmosphere is well re-created musically by Manuel de Falla's Nights in the *Gardens of Spain*.

Moors and Christians

The Moors established their caliphate in the south but their power stretched to every corner of the peninsula. However, Christian kingdoms flourished in the far north and were eventually responsible for the rebellion which became known as the Reconquest. It took Christian troops seven centuries to achieve a definite end to Muslim rule in Spain, a triumph which continues to be celebrated to this day during the *fiesta* known throughout Spain simply as 'Moors and Christians'.

THE COLONIAL PERIOD

When Granada was taken back in 1492, the entire peninsula became unified under Ferdinand and Isabella (known as the Catholic Kings) and something that began to look like the Spain we know today emerged for the first time. An Italian, Peter Martyr, who lived during the reign of the Catholic Kings, wrote: 'Who would have believed that the Galician, the fierce Asturian and the rude inhabitants of the Pyrenees, men accustomed to deeds of atrocious violence, and to brawl and battle on the lightest occasions at home, should mingle amicably, not only with one another, but with the Toledans, the La Manchans and the wily and jealous Andalusians; all living together in

Christopher Columbus points the way to the New World from Barcelona.

harmonious subordination to authority, like members of one family.'

Expulsion of Moors and Jews

Unifying Spain was one of the greatest achievements of the Catholic Kings. However, the expulsion of the cultured Moors and the rich and industrious Jews left great gaps in the agricultural and administrative expertise of Spain. The Moors had been mainly responsible for the intricate terraces and irrigation systems which had created the exotic gardens and fruitful fields and orchards we still marvel at today, and the Jews had been highly placed in court circles as advisers. Without the Moors and the Jews, Spain suffered from a decline in agriculture and the judiciary.

However, an enormous empire came into being soon after Christopher Columbus discovered America.

THE GOLDEN AGE

In 1519, Charles I became Holy Roman Emperor Charles V, marking the birth of the Habsburg dynasty. His accession to the throne also signalled the beginning of Spain's 'Golden Century'. During his reign, Cortés, Pizarro and the *conquistadores* won a whole continent. The New World provided untold wealth to Spain and culture flourished in the Spanish court and noble houses. The most advanced artistic schools of Europe were encouraged to visit Spain. They produced an architectural and artistic heritage hard to equal anywhere else in the world.

The Inquisition

Philip II, Charles' son, succeeded him in 1558. Alarmed by the spread of Protestantism, he increased the scope and ferocity of the Inquisition which imprisoned thousands of 'heretics'. Hundreds were burned at the stake during the frequent *autos-da-fé*. The Jews who had not been expelled and had 'converted' to Catholicism were often suspected of practising their former religion in secret and suffered many violent punishments.

The Armada

Spanish harbours in the New World, as well as international trade, were constantly being harassed by English 'pirates'. This eventually led Philip to raise a powerful fleet to invade England. This venture ended in the defeat of the Great Armada in 1588.

Philip spent the closing years of his life in monastic austerity at the huge Escorial he had planned and constructed on the bleak windswept slopes of the Guadarrama.

The Spanish Inquisition

Instituted in 1480, the Spanish Inquisition was a separate tribunal of the Roman Catholic Church designed to rid the country of *heretics*, i.e. anyone who opposed the teachings of the Church. Its primary tenets were:

- to offer protection to converted Jews called *conversos* from retaliation by hostile members of the Jewish faith and to make sure they did not return to Judaism.
- to seek out false converts called *marranos*, Jews who continued to practise their faith in private.
- to prevent the relapse of converted Moors called *moriscos* and their alliance with heretical groups

17th-century Painters

The 17th century was Spain's 'golden age' of painting. Devotional artists of different characters flourished; for example, the ascetic Francisco de Zurbarán, the gentle Bartolomé Esteban Murillo and the Greek immigrant known simply as El Greco. This century also produced the first of Spain's indigenous universal geniuses—Diego Rodriguez de Silva Velasquez. If you are interested not only in Spanish but also in European culture, the Velasquez rooms at the Prado in Madrid are a must.

SPAIN'S DECLINE

The vast but distant empire in the New World was too difficult to govern from Spain. In the 18th century, the Habsburg dynasty was replaced by the Bourbons. By the 19th century, the only remaining colonies were Cuba, Puerto Rico, the Philippines and some parts of Africa.

First Constitution

Liberal ideas had an early start in Spain: the country drew up its first constitution in 1812. Conservatives and Liberals, although fighting each other over the new ideologies spreading throughout Europe, made peace in order to rid themselves of Napoleonic troops. (Napoleon's brother Joseph was made king of Spain in 1808.) Once independence was achieved, however, they were at it again and the 19th century reflected the turmoil experienced elsewhere in Europe.

What are you?

If asked "What are you?" most people will answer "I am English or American or French…" and then proceed to specify "I come from Devon or Florida or Normandy…" ending up with "My home town is Exeter or Miami or Cherbourg…" The Spaniard, on the other hand, will reverse this order and start with "I am from Denia" (most important), "I am Valencian" (of secondary interest) and, if pressed further, will admit "Oh yes, I am Spanish." The Spaniard's individualism is reflected in this peculiar identification with the local area rather than the country as a whole. Such an attitude could be a result of the pronounced differences between the regions.

Anyone coming from outside Spain is an *extranjero* but even a Spaniard from the next village will be referred to as a *forastero* (stranger). To this day, Spaniards retain this extreme individualism.

THE 20TH CENTURY

At the end of the 19th century, Spain had lost most of its remaining colonies in a war with the United States. The country began to suffer from an identity crisis. Several generations had witnessed tremendous political changes with no stability in sight. The Second Republic was declared in 1931 but civil war broke out five years later.

Francisco Franco

For nearly four decades, Francisco Franco—born in 1893— was a significant if not dominant figure in the life of Spain, maintaining his resistance to the modern world even as his health started failing in the early 1970s. Eisenhower sent Vernon Walters to find out what Franco was planning for his succession. His message to the President was "When I am gone, I will leave a Spain that has a restored monarchy, a professional army subordinate to the civilian democratic government and a strong and vibrant middle class" which is exactly what he did.

General Franco of the Nationalist forces finally defeated the other factions and put down the rebellion. From his victory in 1939 until the mid-fifties, Spain became internationally isolated. The term 'dictator' brings to mind a ruthless, self-seeking personality, and most of Europe considered Franco to be just that. However, under his regime, law and order was restored and, when he died in 1975, many Spaniards mourned his passing. Foreigners who chose to settle in Spain in those days also benefited from a somewhat outdated constitution which gave them tremendous value for money, practically no crime to fear and a variety of lifestyles to choose from. After Franco's death, the crime rate increased dramatically and houses which previously had been left unlocked and untended for hours at a time, now had to be barred and bolted against intruders.

Life After Franco

Spain was declared a monarchy in 1947, with a king to be named to succeed Franco. In 1969, Franco named the exiled Prince Juan Carlos I de Borbon as his successor and heir to the vacant Spanish throne. Franco died in 1975 and King Juan Carlos, having sworn to uphold Francoist ideals during Franco's lifetime, immediately started to initiate democratic reform. He managed to guide Spain towards political liberalisation, aided by the new Prime Minister Adolfo Suarez Gonzalez.

King Juan Carlos I is a modest monarch who runs a modest household and pays income tax like everyone else. In February 1981, he managed to suppress a rebellion of army generals when Lieutenant Colonel Antonio Tejero Molina of the Guardia Civil walked into the Cortes (the Spanish parliament) brandishing a pistol. His firm and immediate appeal to the army to remain loyal to him as commander-in-chief proved that the new democracy was strong enough to withstand a military coup. When he appeared on television in his army uniform, the whole nation knew they now had a leader who would take them confidently and safely into the 21st century.

SPAIN TODAY

Because of its eventful history, Spanish society is very varied and interesting. Today's Spain now benefits from a stable government and its entrance into the European Economic Community in 1985 signalled its return to the mainstream of continental life. In 1986, Spain also joined the European Union but problems still continue with the threat of terrorism from the Basque Fatherland and Liberty (ETA) and high unemployment rates.

THE HISTORY OF RELIGION

Catholicism has been a strong force in the history of the country since it was declared the sole religion by the Romans in AD 380. During the Middle Ages, when Spain was made up of several kingdoms, religion was the unifying force that held them together. This unity persisted over long periods of crusading along the Iberian peninsula and culminated in the reign of the Catholic Kings who gained complete control over both religion and government. They instituted the cruel, relentless crusade called the Spanish Inquisition which was only abolished in the 1830s.

In 1540, St Ignatius of Loyola founded the Jesuit religious order and sparked the Counter-Reformation—a period of intense Catholic piety that was to dominate Spanish life for many centuries.

However, shortly after it started, it was accused of numerous abuses. Accusations of heresy ran rampant and innocent people were unjustly punished by public trial and condemnation which usually took the form of strangulation or burning at the stake at the frequent *autos-da-fé*. Some Christian groups were sentenced to life imprisonment. Jews and Muslims were either expelled or forced to convert to Catholicism.

In 1931, Catholicism was renounced by the Republic but the Franco years restored its privileges making it the only religion to have legal status. No Protestant church, Jewish synagogue or Muslim mosque was allowed to advertise its services, own property or publish literature. Religious instruction was mandatory in all schools. Many artists and intellectuals left Spain during these years to escape Franco's repressive church-state.

Roman Catholicism is still the major religion of Spain today although the present constitution guarantees religious freedom to all. Roughly 94 per cent of the population identify themselves as Catholic. The remainder belong mainly to Protestant groups, Jehovah's Witnesses and Mormonism, with small communities of Jews in the big cities and Muslims near the southern coast.

THE SPANISH

CHAPTER 3

'An ounce of blood is worth more
than a pound of friendship.'
—Spanish proverb (anon)

Sᴘᴀɪɴ ʜᴀs ᴀ ᴘᴏᴘᴜʟᴀᴛɪᴏɴ ᴏꜰ roughly 40 million people distributed unevenly around the country. Since the 1950s, more than five million have left the poorer rural regions and small towns of the south and west for the more industrialised areas around Madrid, Barcelona, Bilbao and Valencia. Quite a few have gone to work in more prosperous countries such as Switzerland, France and Germany.

Spaniards come from diverse ethnic and linguistic groups whose struggles for recognition have sometimes been disruptive. Repressed during much of the Franco years, regional communities were only granted more recognition in the Constitution of 1978 which guaranteed autonomy for the diverse groups.

AN ETHNIC MIXTURE

Catalans represent 17 per cent of the population, Basques make up 2 per cent and Galicians, or Gallegos, 7 per cent. Other ethic groups include Valencianos, Navarrese, Aragonese and gypsies.

The Catalans

The provinces of Barcelona, Lerida, Tarragona and Gerona make up Catalonia but there are also Catalan-speaking communities in the Balearic Islands, parts of Valencia and also Aragon.

The region became part of a united Spain during the reign of the Catholic Kings. Much later, during the Spanish civil war, a proud 'Catalan Republic' came into existence but it did not survive the Franco years. Autonomy, however, never ceased to be an issue. Loyalty to Catalonia and its culture, and the ability to speak the language, distinguishes the Catalans from other Spaniards.

All students must be bilingual and, in fact, more subjects are taught in Catalan than in Castilian. Catalans are noted for their business acumen, entrepreneurial skills and thriftiness, and the whole region is not only prosperous but industrialised and urbanised.

The Basques

The provinces of Avala, Vizcaya and Guipuzcoa make up the Basque country but how this remote region was settled in the first place remains a mystery. However, the Basques are clearly among the earliest people to inhabit Europe. By nature, they are fiercely independent, proud of both their difficult language called *Euzkera* and their own rural culture.

In the 20th century, Franco tried to repress Basque culture, especially their language, which was fiercely opposed by the people. Today, the Basque spirit of defiance lives on. The worst aspect of this defiance is terrorist violence by separatist groups fighting for total independence from the Spanish government. Even so, the Basque region is one of the more prosperous in Spain with metal, steel and shipbuilding industries attracting migrant workers from the central and southern regions.

The Galicians

In the north-western corner of Spain, the provinces of La Coruna, Lugo, Orense and Ponteverde make up the region known as Galicia. The inhabitants are descended from early Celtic invaders who came from northern Europe and settled in Galicia between 1,000–600 BC. During the Middle Ages, a short-lived kingdom did exist but the southern part eventually became Portugal, leaving the northern part in complete disorder until 1483 when it was incorporated into the kingdom of Castile. The region is sparsely populated because in the 20th century, almost one million people left Galicia to seek their fortunes elsewhere in Spain.

Modern-day nationalist movements date from 1931 but Galician efforts for autonomy are less aggressive than the demands of Catalans and Basques. Galicians, by nature and tradition, tend to be shepherds, farmers or fishermen, and their rural lifestyle keeps them from achieving the wealth and education of Spaniards who live in more urbanised areas.

The Gypsies

It is thought that gypsies migrated from Iran or India to Europe as early as the 11th century, arriving in Spain in the 1400s where they were rather well received. Circumstances changed during the Spanish Inquisition and they were persecuted along with the Moors and the Jews. Persecution continued and gypsies were still considered inferior in the 1980s. More recently, efforts have been made to bring them into mainstream Spanish and European society by promoting education in their communities. Care is taken not to destroy their rich and distinctive cultural traditions, particularly their passionate singing and dancing which have charmed audiences worldwide.

Gypsy Superstitions

Perhaps because of their reputation for being able to cast an 'evil eye', gypsies are avoided by most Spaniards who are reluctant to get involved with them. Even when it is known that they are responsible for small household burglaries, such misdemeanors tend to be tolerated by the rest of the community in order not to provoke retaliation.

There are two distinct groups of gypsies in Spain. The first are *gitanos* who are to be found in central and southern Spain, making their living as street entertainers or vendors. The second are *hungaros*, who live a more nomadic lifestyle in temporary tents and shacks on city fringes, and are generally poorer than the *gitanos*.

You will see more gypsies in the south of Spain, mainly Andalusia. Traditionally a nomadic people, they do not hold regular jobs and many of them turn to begging or petty thievery.

CATHOLIC INFLUENCES

Although Protestant churches in Spain are now treated equally, for centuries, Spain has been a strongly Catholic country with the Church and priests playing a big part in the everyday life of the average citizen. Most Spaniards are baptised, married and buried by the Church. The Roman Catholic Church did not recognise divorce and prohibited the use of contraceptives. These restrictions have resulted in Spanish families being very large, with strong ties among siblings. Today, however, both divorce and the use of contraceptives are legal and economic considerations, together with the process of urbanisation, tend to limit the size of families.

Extended Families

In the 1950s and 1960s, millions of Spaniards migrated from rural to urban areas. At that time, accommodation was scarce and because family ties have always been strong in Spain, several generations often lived together, sharing one house or flat. Perhaps this is why extended families are the norm rather than the exception in Spain. In the old days, families were very close-knit, spending weekends together and usually sharing at least two meals together. These days the young people, although they may live at home until they get married, spend more time out with their friends than at home with their families. Homes for the elderly called *Residencias* are also becoming more common, with construction being taken on by regional governments as well as the private sector.

The extended family is still very common in Spain and you will find households where several generations still live together.

Spain's Little Treasures

VS Pritchett described Spanish women as being passionate lovers of children and claimed that there was marriage and eight children in their eyes. This was true in the old days when birth control was frowned upon and Spanish families tended to be large. Contraception was illegal and the birth rate remained high until the mid-1970s when it fell dramatically. Modern couples (especially those in the cities) now realise the importance of family planning and have fewer children.

Spanish children have always been treated like little princes and princesses. More money is lavished on their little suits and beautiful dresses than on their parents' clothing. They are obviously loved and pampered, even overindulged at times.

This indulgence becomes evident in the way Spaniards quite happily accept the presence of tiny babies and small children in restaurants, irrespective of the time of day or night. When you take your family to a restaurant, don't be surprised if the waiter whisks your little darling off into the kitchen to be admired by the rest of the staff.

Even the smallest village will have a park with facilities for children such as swings, slides and sandpits. If you have small children, find a park near to where you live and make a point of taking your children to play there. You may find it hard-going trying to communicate with other parents at first, but your children will soon start chattering to other youngsters. This is one of the easiest ways to meet people and make friends in Spain.

In a big city with no public park nearby, the same result can be achieved simply by taking your child (or even dog) for a walk... you will soon meet Spaniards who are out walking with their child or dog and before long compliments and comparisons will be exchanged.

Spain's King Juan Carlos and Queen Sofia are welcomed by Mallorca's Bishop Jesus Murgui before the traditional Mass of the Resurrection in Palma de Mallorca on 23 March 2008.

To Spaniards, bullfighting is an art form comparable to ballet—bullfight in the Plaza de Toros in Madrid.

The Sagrada Familia designed by Antonia Gaudi stands as one of the most famous icons of Barcelona.

Spain has a number of world-renowned buildings such as the Guggenheim Museum in Bilbao designed by American architect Frank Gehry.

Rolling green fields showcase the beauty of the countryside, Andalusia, Spain.

The splendour of Catalonia Chair Light in Montserrat Monastery Chapel attests to Spain's rich cultural heritage.

SOCIALISING

CHAPTER 4

'Life without a friend is like death without a witness.'
—Spanish proverb (anon)

LIFESTYLES VARY CONSIDERABLY depending on where you choose to reside. How quickly you fit in will depend on a number of factors, chief amongst them is the answer to the question 'How adaptable are you?'.

THE LOVE OF SOCIALISING
Spaniards love to gather together and talk, and you will see groups of old men sitting in bars, talking and playing cards or dominoes, or sitting in the village square, chatting.

Spaniards are a gregarious people, generally vivacious, ready to enjoy a party and join in celebrations. They are passionate about their family, their faith and the arts, but also enjoy modest pleasures such as a good meal, a sunny courtyard full of flowers, friends and a hearty laugh. The women will gather on doorsteps to exchange the latest news and gossip, and family groups consisting of several generations can often be seen partying together. However, you may be surprised to find that Spaniards do most of their socialising out of doors, or else in bars and cafes. They very seldom entertain even their own friends in their homes.

SOCIAL CUSTOMS AND ETIQUETTE
Spanish Surnames
Surnames can be extremely confusing due to the fact that the mother's name is added on to the full name, so that in effect the middle name is the surname. For example, should

your name be John James Smith, Spaniards will assume that your surname is James and Smith is simply your mother's surname. Listings in phone books should therefore be checked carefully or you could find yourself listed under one of your Christian names! Spanish women do not change their surnames when they get married.

Manners and Mannerisms

Mannerisms and social behaviour are both influenced by the Spanish temperament which, as has been mentioned before, is strongly individualistic. In a general way, Spaniards are one of the most formally polite of all people. Remember this when you are making introductions. However, do not take offence if you are not introduced to all the people in a room or at your table... it may merely be that your name is too difficult to pronounce correctly! In such cases, it is quite in order for you to introduce yourself.

Certain Formalities

When meeting a Spaniard for the first time, it is a good idea to be as formal as possible. You should introduce yourself in detail, tell him who you are, where you come from and what you are doing in Spain. In return, he will welcome you expansively and tell you to feel at home. Only after such formalities have been exchanged will casual and friendly conversation start to take place.

Forms of Address

When addressing a Spaniard, *Señor* (Mr), *Señora* (Mrs) or *Señorita* (Miss) should be prefixed to the surname of the person to whom you are speaking. On better acquaintance, you may use *Don* (male) or *Doña* (female) with the Christian name. Nowadays, Christian names alone are quite

A Sense of Humour

Spaniards may take offence if you pass critical comments about their country or their customs. Even if you intend your remarks to be taken as a joke, be careful what you say, and to whom. For example, the Guardia Civil used to wear plastic-looking black triangular hats. A foreign friend asked one why his hat was such a funny shape, and was lucky that this particular Guardia had a sense of humour. He replied, with a twinkle in his eye, that the unusual design allowed him to relax leaning against a wall without his hat falling off!

acceptable amongst the younger generation. Incidentally, wedding rings are worn on the fourth finger of the right hand, rather than the fourth finger of the left hand. If you are in doubt about the status of a woman, a quick glance at her right hand should clarify whether to address her as *Señora* or *Señorita*.

Evening Paseo

Visitors to Spain are sometimes surprised to find towns and villages which appear completely devoid of humans. However, when the magic hour of the evening *paseo* (stroll) arrives, you may well wonder where all the people sprang from. In some towns, the *paseo* takes place in the main square. In some cities, it could occur along an esplanade. At around seven o'clock in the evening, you will notice a few freshly-showered, well-dressed young women, chatting animatedly together (rarely with a man) and walking sedately in twos and threes. More and more people begin appearing, including children and grandparents and an informal parade around the square or up and down the Ramblas takes place.

The evening *paseo* is a time for leisurely politeness and mild flirtation. Although the girls are in effect 'displaying' themselves, they do so proudly and seldom allow their eyes to meet those of a man. Tradition dictates that a certain amount of care is taken with one's dress: you would not be too popular if you chose to join a *paseo* coming straight from the beach. In the coolness of a summer evening, joining a *paseo* is a pleasant way of taking gentle exercise and working up an appetite for the evening meal. For the older generation of Spaniard, this may well be the only form of 'exercise' they enjoy.

Kissing

Expect a handshake when you are being introduced but do not be surprised if you get kissed on both cheeks when you leave a party or any social gathering. This is quite normal in Spain. Women will kiss the men and the other women, but men will only kiss women. A man may give another man a big hug but it is just an expression of friendly feeling, nothing more!

In this connection, a young American married to a Spaniard told me: "It has become so natural to hug or kiss everyone and their mother-in-law; an old boyfriend from my student days and his new girlfriend; a neighbour's visiting brother; a business associate's wife… that when I go home to

California on holiday, the people there seem very standoffish, and I have to curb my impulse to pass out hugs and kisses freely."

Sneezing
It may come as a bit of a shock to hear a loud *'Jesus'* after you have sneezed but this is simply the Spanish equivalent of 'Bless you'. In Spain, the name Jesus crops up almost as frequently as Jose or Jaime and is often included in the name of a village. Foreigners may find it strange to see a village with a signpost saying *'Jesus Pobre'* ('Poor Jesus').

Dropping In
Before telephones became more easily available, dropping in was the accepted way of communicating with one's friends. Late morning or early evening were the usual times when refreshments could be offered and accepted. Now that most homes have telephones, this habit of dropping in has become almost obsolete since it is a simple matter to pick up your phone and invite your friends to whatever entertainment you have in mind. Should you find it necessary to drop in, make sure you avoid the post-lunch period when many people still enjoy a *siesta*.

Visiting Homes
Spaniards rarely entertain in their own homes, usually preferring to do so at a favourite restaurant. Should you be honoured with an invitation to a Spanish home for lunch or dinner, a small gift may be appropriate—chocolates, flowers or wine. When you have a meal in someone's home, you will find that the hosts will keep offering you 'a little more'. They will be very insistent and you should, in fact, accept a little more or they will think you don't like the food they are serving. It's a sort of game they play, but a fattening one!

Foreigners in Spain, on the other hand, often prefer to entertain their friends at home rather than in restaurants. You will find that your Swedish friends will nearly always arrive with a bunch of flowers from the garden or a prettily wrapped bottle of wine. You may find yourself receiving a

Spanish table manners decree that you should keep both hands clearly visible above the table at all times.

small gift if your guest feels unable to return your hospitality within a reasonable period of time. This is a tradition not so common amongst the British, except on 'special' occasions such as birthday or Christmas parties.

Children are usually welcome wherever you go and are almost always included in parties. However, if you are invited to a Spanish home for the first time for a specific meal, don't bring the children unless they are invited. Once the Spanish family knows you and your children, you will find that your children will be included in most invitations.

Birthdays

Children have birthday parties arranged for them by their parents, and quite lavish ones on occasion. They invite lots of little friends who arrive with presents, and the parents organise games and distribute cakes and drinks. For adults, however, it is the reverse. The birthday boy or girl is expected to invite his/her friends, co-workers or classmates out for a drink or meal to celebrate his/her birthday. It needn't be more than a get-together over a cup of coffee or a drink, but if it's your birthday, you are the host.

Dressing for the Occasion

Once again, you will find Spaniards tend to be more formal than most other nations. In hot weather, of course, the dress will be more casual than in the winter months, but strapless tops may not be appreciated even in the middle of a heat wave, nor collarless T-shirts for men. When visiting government departments or any office in general, it is advisable to dress correctly.

In coastal resort areas, dress has become more and more casual. It is not unusual to find tourists wandering about in supermarkets wearing scanty bikinis. This behaviour may be tolerated in some areas but is not recommended if you intend to become a resident.

You will soon be able to recognise a Spaniard at a glance because even when they are dressed 'informally' they are usually immaculately turned out. In cities like Madrid, the women are very clothes-conscious and fashion is of supreme importance. They will spend huge amounts of money buying dresses and accessories just to keep up with the latest fashion trends.

Appropriate Dressing

A friend went to the customs office to see the man in charge and found himself being ushered in ahead of others sitting in the waiting room. As he was leaving, he could not resist asking why he had received this preferential treatment since he had not made an appointment. The answer startled him: 'If these people do not have the courtesy to dress in a respectful manner, they can wait all day...' The people considered to be disrespectfully dressed included a man wearing a pair of shorts rather than long trousers, and another wearing flip-flops instead of shoes.

COURTSHIP AND WEDDINGS

Very attentive during courtship, the Spanish male appears extremely romantic and willing to do practically anything to win the favour of his beloved. He wants to sweep the girl off her feet and carry her off to his 'castle'; but once he has succeeded, the relationship is likely to change.

Big or small, Spanish weddings will normally include some form of meal and your wedding gift is expected to

A suit and tie are appropriate for all occasions, even when riding a scooter.

be worth more than the meal you will be offered. About 30 euros per person would be considered adequate in Madrid, less in smaller towns and villages. All the usual wedding gifts, such as silver, linen, crystal, even kitchen appliances, are appropriate. Wedding lists exist in cities, larger urban communities and even in some of the smaller villages. If a wedding list has been made, you will be informed of the name of the shop handling it.

Marriage

Beautiful church weddings are the climax of many a girl's existence and her moment of glory; but once she is installed in her 'castle', it may at times, seem more like a prison. From being a pampered and spoilt *novia* (fiancée/bride), she soon becomes a hard-working housewife whose duties consist of producing and caring for babies, and generally taking care of house and home, husband and family. In the old days, the husband was treated like a king and his merest whim was catered to. He was served first at meal times and often left the table before the rest of the family had finished eating. He was never expected to lift a finger in the running of the house, but wandered off to spend time with his male cronies, drinking *carajillos* (coffee laced with brandy or anise) and playing dominoes in some bar. To this day you will still find groups of men gathering in bars solely for this purpose.

'Second-Class Citizens'

Foreign girls marrying Spaniards were often surprised at the change of attitude which rapidly took place after the wedding. Their doting *novios* (fiancés/grooms) suddenly reversed the pre-marriage roles and expected to be waited on hand and foot. In the past, women in Spain were very definitely second-class citizens. They seldom aspired to being more than a housewife, and very few tackled advanced studies and careers in business or politics. This has, of course, changed radically in recent years, particularly in urban and coastal areas. Many married women now hold a regular job, either for financial reasons or for self-fulfilment. Among younger couples, husbands help with the housework and also look after the children, just as in other developed countries.

Divorce

Divorce did not exist until recent times. Marriages were made to last a lifetime and, even to this day, a divorce takes at least two years to be finalised. You have to establish the fact that you have been living apart for two years if the separation was mutually agreed upon, or five years if it was not. Otherwise, you have to start the proceedings by obtaining a legal separation and either partner is free to petition for divorce after one year has elapsed.

SEX AND MORALITY

In modern-day Spain, objecting to sex is considered by some to be as taboo as condoning it was in the past. In the last ten to 15 years, women's attitude to sex has changed dramatically. In the old days, they were brought up to play the

Tortura de la Galanteria

Translated, this means 'the torture of compliments and attention'. Spanish men tend to be very vocal with women, even those they do not know. Do not be offended if you hear loud comments as you walk by... they are usually complimentary, more or less the equivalent of the American 'wolf whistle'.

piano and also to play second fiddle to their husbands, doing everything in their power to further his career. Nowadays, many women prefer to have careers of their own and they have turned to professions such as medicine and law. This has made them more demanding, open and authentic in their behaviour. No longer is it 'wrong' to talk about sex with friends and family. No longer do women consider orgasm a sin and a sure way of becoming pregnant.

A divorced woman used to be called a 'black duck' (the equivalent of a black sheep) and shunned by her family and friends. These days, many Spaniards get divorced and no longer are they treated as pariahs. Husbands were always (and still are) expected to be unfaithful but these days, the wives are likely to be equally as unfaithful!

As a general rule, Spaniards will treat you with astonishing courtesy, but remember that family ties are very strong. Spanish men may treat their women as second-class citizens and expect unquestioning love and devotion, but in return they will protect their women totally and will spring to their defence if there is any question of their honour being insulted in any way. Young foreigners should be careful how they approach Spanish girls who may have unusually sensitive and aggressive brothers or boyfriends nearby. Knives have been known to flash if a Spaniard becomes provoked.

A Sense of Honour

Although the word *machismo* originated in Mexico, it is a product of Mexico's Spanish heritage. The 'macho' concept involves a code of moral values centred on a peculiar conception of honour—honour which can be lost either by one's own actions or those of one's relatives.

Modesty is a thing of the past for many Spanish women but nearly all still place a tremendous importance on appearance. Wherever you go, you will find that Spanish women are greatly concerned about being well dressed. More and more young women work outside their homes and spend their money on the latest fashions.

SPANISH NEIGHBOURS

If you live in a block of flats in one of the larger cities and have Spanish neighbours, you will probably become close friends in due course. But, if you live in an urbanisation, it may be more difficult to make friends with the people occupying the other houses. However, in most instances, should there be any form of 'emergency', no matter how minor, your Spanish neighbour will leap at the opportunity to help in any way possible.

For example, should you suddenly develop a violent pain in your stomach and retire to your bed wondering how to get hold of a doctor, your partner only needs to mention your 'problem' to your Spanish neighbours before you find yourself being overwhelmed by their 'attentions'. Not only will they, if necessary, send their son running to fetch a doctor, but they themselves are quite likely to wander into your bedroom to assess your condition and offer sympathy in the form of a bottle of whisky.

RESPECTING SPANISH PRIVACY

Homes are very private affairs in Spain. Unlike 'townhouses' found in other parts of the world which usually have a small front garden and a bit of a backyard, providing perfect opportunities for neighbours to exchange friendly chatter over their fences, a townhouse in Spain will have neither. A glance through the large and heavy front doors will usually be rewarded by the sight of attractive inner courtyards, full of greenery and pots of flowers and, occasionally, a fountain tinkling away. The home is the domain of the Spanish housewife who, whether working or not, diligently cares for home and family.

However, don't be surprised to find Spaniards gathering on the pavement in front of their houses to exchange the latest 'news' whilst enjoying the evening breeze in summer or the last rays of sunshine in winter.

Foreigners are often puzzled by the Spanish preference for 'street socialising' rather than 'at home socialising'. This, however, encourages neighbours and local residents to get to know one another more intimately. You will find yourself being politely greeted should you stroll past such an outdoor gathering. Here's your chance to practise your Spanish by exchanging a few pleasantries!

Older people like to meet in the park for a game of chess or dominoes.

Townhouses have become increasingly popular with foreigners as they offer far more security than villas set in gardens in an urbanisation. They are also much more economical to maintain and easier to run.

DOMESTIC HELP

In the old days, many families could afford a string of servants and retainers. Nowadays, most households are satisfied if they can have a cleaning woman come once or twice a week, and even these are becoming rarer now. The younger generation of Spanish women would far rather get a 'proper job' if they have enough education; even serving in a supermarket is far more appealing than cleaning someone else's silver.

However, it must be added that Spanish homes are immaculate. Housewives are extremely house-proud and devote themselves to maintaining a very high standard of cleanliness and tidiness.

Strangely enough, the sparkling cleanliness in the Spanish home is not duplicated in the streets. These tend to be littered with paper wrappers, cigarette butts and even discarded bits of food. An effort to improve this situation has caused numerous rubbish bins to appear in strategic places in most public areas. Even if the locals still throw their rubbish on the street, you should use the bins provided.

JOINING CLUBS

Some clubs are exceptionally expensive. A recent survey put Spain at the top of the list, the annual fee for a tennis club being the highest in Europe. Golf clubs and yacht clubs are all pricey to join, no doubt because their inability to expand, due to lack of space, may require them to limit their membership numbers. Some clubs are very exclusive and the typical Spanish reluctance to say 'no' outright may raise your hopes of acceptance. Your name will be put on a waiting list but you may find yourself waiting indefinitely. However, if you do join a club, you will certainly find it a good way to meet Spaniards and other foreigners with interests similar to your own. Joining gardening societies or philatelic clubs can be achieved at almost no cost, and there are amateur theatrical groups in most places.

Children have clubs which promote the same kind of community spirit as the boy scouts or girl guides. Most of the cities, towns and even villages have well-equipped parks, and there are zoos, amusement and safari parks to be visited. In Barcelona, 'Catalunya in Miniature' comprises 60,000 sq m (72,000 sq yds) of the province's most famous buildings, including the complete works of Gaudi all scaled down and the Parc Guell is a very popular playground for the city's children.

MAKING FRIENDS

Having settled in the area of your choice and made efforts to adapt to your surroundings, will you now be able to make

Do Your Homework

Should you find yourself in an area where domestic help is available and are confronted by a Spanish woman eager to offer her services, one of the things you should make very clear right from the start is exactly what her duties will encompass. The pay is usually so many euros per hour and it would be wise to check around your suburb or village to find out what the local rate is. If you agree to pay more than the accepted local rate, you might find yourself very unpopular with the other residents!

Spaniards liven up their balconies with potted plants and bright flowers.

lots of friends? The answer is yes, but not perhaps as many Spanish friends as you might like.

Spaniards have a reputation for being 'private people' and this is still true to a degree, particularly with the older generation who are likely to have more formulated likes and dislikes. Young people tend to be more open and forthcoming, but boys, in particular, can be hostile at times. Some may get involved in gangs of different nationalities whose rivalry can escalate to incidents requiring police intervention.

As already mentioned, the Spaniards are very private, and for centuries women were kept at home and very much in the background. Even if you can speak Spanish and the local variety at that, you may find it disappointing that you are not welcomed into Spanish homes with open arms. Your friends may entertain you at a restaurant, they will be happy to play golf or tennis with you or take you boating, but you will seldom be asked to enter their home. This is true of all the areas, although perhaps the urban Spaniard,

Although Spaniards are very home-proud people, they rarely invite friends home. Instead they prefer to meet you in a restaurant or café.

being more sophisticated in many ways, is more likely to open his house to you.

What it boils down to in the end is 'How much effort are you prepared to make?' Unless you are willing to immerse yourself in the Spanish lifestyle, chances are you will eventually want to return to your home country.

On the other hand, "I was lucky," writes one American. "I came when I was 20 with a friend. We ignored the 'great American buffalo herd' and went off travelling and playing on our own. We adapted quickly. Within a month, we'd been out with bullfighters and soldiers, doctors and clerks, and even home to meet some of their families and all of their friends. Spain is lots of fun if you make an effort to get to know the people."

Most foreigners admit that although it may not be difficult to make friends, making 'close' friends is a different matter. "Even though I speak Spanish fluently, there always seems to be some sort of barrier which impedes a close friendship," says another American.

ALTERNATIVE LIFESTYLES

For the purposes of this book, Spain can be divided into three basic regional areas: urban, rural and coastal. The coastal regions can be further divided into coastal urban and coastal rural. The contrast between these areas is very marked and they offer the widest imaginable range of lifestyles.

Urban

The cities reflect the province in which they are found and carry the same name as the province. Since there are 17 autonomous communities in Spain, cities tend to have their own individual identity. For the foreigner looking for a city in which to reside, the choice is wide.

Barcelona in the industrial north, big and bustling and proudly Catalan, is full of ancient Gothic architectural treasures, as well as modern buildings, well-stocked supermarkets, luxury shops and large department stores.

Seville in southernmost Andalusia is very different, with a strong Moorish influence. The old Jewish Quarter, the Barrio

San Sebastian in the Basque province bears a close resemblance to the French Riviera.

de Santa Cruz, with its whitewashed houses, patios and balconies full of flowers, cobbled squares and twisting alleys is beautifully preserved.

By contrast, San Sebastian in the Basque country on the north Atlantic coast has none of the flamboyance of southern Spain. Laid out in a very modern way, it is now a seaside resort on a par with Monte Carlo or Nice.

Rural

Even though there are many highly cosmopolitan cities in Spain, a large proportion of the Iberian peninsula is still very rural. Enormous tracts of interior are devoted to agriculture. Grains, olives and, of course, vineyards in the central part of the country are a major source of wealth. Here can be found tiny medieval villages operating quite possibly without running water, electricity and telephones. Plains bordering the Mediterranean are extremely fertile. Always green, they are famous for their orange and lemon groves. Almond orchards provide spectacular shows of pink and white blossoms in the early part of the year. Fields south of Valencia produce vast quantities of the round-grain rice favoured for *paella* and they have even started to produce the long-grain variety.

Coastal

The various *costas* (literally meaning 'coasts' or 'shores') originally consisted of small seaside fishing villages. Many of the villages during the past two decades have been developed at great cost into international resorts. There are six *costas* situated between the conservative Costa Brava north of Barcelona and the 'jet set' ambience of the Costa Del Sol in the south. Midway between these two, the Costa Blanca—popular with retired couples from all over the world—claims to have the 'best climate in all of Europe'.

Resorts

The rapid development along the Mediterranean coast, spurred on by the ever-increasing numbers of tourists flooding in during the summer months of July and August, has created a lifestyle of its own. Places like Benidorm, which were quiet beauty spots before the tourist boom, now cater to thousands of happy visitors during the season. Towering blocks of flats overlook the two lovely sandy beaches barely visible under the blanket of humanity spread over them.

Crowded and Maddening

Be warned! If 'Far from the Madding Crowd' is your concept of the ideal, avoid Benidorm. As a general rule, the resorts are crowded with holiday makers from all over Europe.

The Ballearics

These islands are a combination of coastal urban and coastal rural. Halfway between France and Africa off Spain's Mediterranean coast, Majorca, Minorca, Ibiza and Formentera became an autonomous province in 1983, but in many ways they remain independent of one another. Castilian Spanish was replaced on each island by a local Catalan dialect making sign posts and road signs here incredibly confusing.

Majorca

By far the largest of the islands, Majorca has a reputation for cheap package tours. This, however, is mostly confined to coastal areas. Inland you will find deserted monasteries, small museums, bird sanctuaries, caves and charming villages—all relatively unspoilt and full of character.

Minorca

The surprising thing about Minorca is its 'Englishness', the result of its century of British rule. Prehistoric monuments dot the landscape but its Georgian-style buildings and small tidy fields make it quite different from the rest of Spain. The language itself is peppered with English words. Franco punished this republican island after the Civil War by restricting tourism, but this was in effect a bonus—no high-rise hotels!

Ibiza and Formentera

Transformed by tourism from a mainly peasant society into a wild anything-goes type of place, the principal resort of San Antonio is now looked upon as one of the noisiest and most brash on the Mediterranean. By way of contrast, peasant women in their simple country costumes can still be seen collecting almonds in their aprons or herding goats.

The Canary Islands

Just north of the Tropic of Cancer, about 150 km (100 miles) off the coast of West Africa, the Canary Islands are a group of seven islands offering warm and sunny climates throughout the year. It is never too hot as the Atlantic sea breezes help to temper the climate. The archipelago became one of the 17 autonomous regions of Spain in 1981. These islands range from the large resort developments on Tenerife and Gran Canarias to the tranquillity and seclusion on the tiny islands of Gomera and Hierro.

There are regular car ferries between the islands and a fast jetfoil service between Tenerife and Gran Canarias. Transport on the islands themselves is generally quite good. Inexpensive taxi services are plentiful with metered fares for

In 1959, the beach at Benidorm (*above*) was a deserted stretch of sand with rolling hills in the background and a sheer cliff dropping to the sea. Today (*below*), you can barely see the sand, and the hills have been levelled out to make way for hotels and skyscrapers.

short trips and 'bargaining' special fares for longer journeys. Bus services, at reasonable rates, are available on most of the islands, with Tenerife and Gran Canarias offering special minibuses called *waa waas*. However, transport on the smaller islands is more limited.

If you are looking for lots of sunshine, Lanzarote and Fuerteventura are most likely to supply it. Fuerteventura has tracts of soft white sand dunes which stretch for miles, allowing a fair amount of privacy which makes it popular with naturists. Tenerife, on the other hand, has small black-pebble beaches whilst Lanzarote is unique with its lunar landscape of volcanic 'badlands'. It is strangely beautiful and is now a national park.

CHURCH AND STATE

The Roman Catholic Church has played an important part in Spain ever since the Christians ousted the Moors and Spain became unified under the Catholic Kings. During the Franco regime, other religions were driven underground and, in a general way, the Church still permeates the lives of most Spaniards, especially in provincial towns. The number of Spaniards in holy orders is still high by any standards. Each village has its priest who is often treated like a member of the family. In some households, no *fiesta* would be complete without the priest presiding at the table.

Religious Freedom

Religious freedom became a constitutional right under King Juan Carlos. Contraceptives are now on open sale and, despite Church protest, even abortions are permitted in certain instances. Spain has now become a secular state although the influence of the Church is still very strong.

First Communion

This still plays a major role in the lives of most Spaniards. First Communion marks the reaffirmation of a Catholic's faith in the Church. Families will spend more on clothes and celebrations, and relatives will come from all over Spain more readily for a First Communion than for any other occasion, including a wedding. If you are invited to a First Communion, a small gift of jewellery of religious significance (medallion, rosary, etc) may be presented to the child. You should behave with decorum as is called for on such an occasion.

Quite An Event!
First Communion celebrations can occur in quite unexpected places. We were once surprised to find about 100 people congregating at our normally deserted mountain *merendero* (small restaurant), quite off the beaten track. It soon became obvious that this was a First Communion celebration, jointly organised by the parents of five or six little girls, all wearing the most beautiful lacy long white dresses. There was singing and feasting... the *paella* was prepared out of doors on a wood fire in a pan measuring more than a metre across with the ingredients and several kilos of rice being stirred around with spades instead of spoons!

Saints' Days

Religion in Spain is not just a Sunday affair. For instance, a typical religious and social custom is to call people up on their saint's day and wish them a happy day. Saints' days are just as important, if not more so, than birthdays. Your saint's day is the feast day of the patron saint whose name you bear. Of course, you have to have a memory similar to that of a computer to record all such important dates in order to comply with this custom! However, if you do remember to call up a friend or colleague on their saint's day, it will be most appreciated.

Shrines and Sanctuaries

What is beautiful to the Spaniard is sometimes seen as rather macabre to the foreigner who may not be used to statues or idols featuring congealed blood. Most of the well-known shrines throughout Spain are home to either a statue of the Virgin or some holy relic. Both the statue and the relic are treated with enormous reverence. The statues of the Virgin frequently have rooms full of beautiful dresses and cloaks, jewellery and ornaments, and their outfits will be changed regularly. These statues and holy relics are paraded with great ceremony once a year on the feast day of the saint. Shrines and sanctuaries are considered holy places and you should treat them with great respect, just like Spaniards do.

The Virgin Mary

Statues of the Virgin Mary abound throughout Spain and most have their shrines in great monasteries which are full of magnificent art treasures. Some of these statues were discovered under miraculous circumstances and are credited with inspiring exceptional bravery by the Christians during their battles against the Moors. The black-faced image of the Virgin known as 'La Morena' at Montserrat is very small, old and dark, quite unimpressive, and yet it can attract as many as 2,000 pilgrims and visitors at any one time. There is even enough room for them all at the monastery, in addition to the Benedictine monks who reside there.

CHURCHES AND CATHEDRALS

Every village has at least one church, usually high on a hill and crowned with a cupola-shaped roof of brilliant tiles, blue for the most part. There are more magnificent cathedrals in Spain than anywhere else in the world, most of them brimming with treasures. Some of the most interesting churches and monasteries include the Cathedral in Seville, the Mezquita in Cordoba, the Convent of Las Duenas in Salamanca and the Temple Expiatiori de la Sagrada Familia in Barcelona.

If the doors are unlocked to any of these holy places, you can safely assume that you can enter. Make sure that you are dressed appropriately (i.e. in formal clothes) before going in. Even if no service is actually in progress, there may be people inside at prayer. Respect them and keep your voice lowered. The church may be brimming with art treasures, but it is not a museum for you to gawk at and exclaim over.

Services

In areas with large foreign communities, church services are available in languages other than Spanish. Times and frequency of services are advertised on notice boards in front of the church.

Religious pictures made of tiles
decorate the walls of many villages.
The Virgin Mary is a favourite.

Going to church on Sunday morning is an integral part of the Spanish lifestyle. Many churches in the towns are modern in architecture.

Some churches have choirs and perhaps a guitar accompaniment, and the singing is exceptionally attractive. In fact, several self-confessed normally non-church-going friends say they now make an effort to go to the local church on Sundays simply to hear the singing, even if this entails sitting through lengthy sermons in a foreign language!

When attending a church service, choose your apparel with care. Men and women are not expected to wear shorts or scanty tops when visiting churches or other religious establishments. Although it used to be customary for women to cover their heads with a scarf or kerchief in church, this is no longer necessary except perhaps in small villages and in less 'sophisticated' areas. The safest bet for men is trousers and a shirt, and for women, a demure dress.

Foreign communities are now allowed the use of local churches where they can hold services in denominations other than Catholic, with their own *padre* (priest). These communities may extend their activities to include money-raising affairs such as Christmas bazaars, partly to cover the cost of their *padre* and partly to act as donations to local deserving charities.

Blessing The House

If you live in a rural area, do not be surprised if the village priest comes a-calling during the week preceding Easter. It is still his custom to visit each and every household in the village to bless the house for the coming year and receive a 'token of appreciation'. The priest will bless some salt and sprinkle your doorstep with holy water and, in return, you are expected to add an egg or two to the basket he carries especially for this purpose. If the basket appears to be too full, a donation of a few euros is a very acceptable alternative. This is a charming custom and refusing entrance to the priest because you are not Catholic will only create tension in the village.

FUNERALS

By law, a burial or cremation should not take place sooner than 24 hours after death. However, it is not customary in Spain to delay a funeral and it will usually take place as soon as possible unless it happens to fall on a *fiesta* or a Sunday. Crematoriums exist in the larger cities. In fact, cremation is becoming acceptable among Spaniards as it has been among northern Europeans—so much so that one coastal council plans to build its own public crematorium in the next phase of expansion.

Funeral insurance is available and recommended as the company, through the local undertaker, takes care of all the paperwork, arranges and pays for the church service, and supplies a coffin, hearse and two wreaths.

Traditionally, the family keep watch by the coffin (at home or in the chapel) all night long and relatives and close family friends are expected to call and keep them company. The length of the visit depends on the closeness of the relationship. As Spaniards are generally demonstrative, tears may be shed and there might by loud wailing and crying amongst the more emotional. However, most Spanish funerals are dignified and solemn.

Cemetaries

These are usually few and set well away from the village houses, enclosed by high walls and surrounded by dark needle-thin cypress trees. Most communities do not bury their dead in the ground. The coffins are slotted into a wall built to house a certain number of coffins. One either buys a niche 'in perpetuity' in which case the coffin will remain in its place as long as any relative remains alive, or the niche is rented for a period of five years. If no further payment is made at the end of five years, the remains will be placed in a common grave. The Spanish attitude towards death can certainly be viewed by some as somewhat casual. The burial walls can be several feet high and, if your coffin is intended for one of the higher niches, it could be hoisted up to the right height by a rickety contraption and then shoved into its hole quite unceremoniously by a Spaniard unconcernedly puffing on a cigar.

All Saints' Day

Celebrated in many parts of Spain as 'the Day of the Dead', 1 November is an occasion when the whole family will try to go to the cemetary to pay their respects. It is not a particularly sad time, enjoying the chance to get together with all their relatives and catch up on family news.

SETTLING IN

CHAPTER 5

'Society is no comfort to one not sociable.'
—William Shakespeare

Noʀтʜ Euʀoᴘᴇᴀɴs ғɪɴᴅ Sᴘᴀɴɪsʜ вuʀᴇᴀuᴄʀᴀᴄʏ a subject for instant conversation. They moan, they marvel, they are outraged. From a north European point of view, the system may appear inefficient, tied up with red tape and possibly corrupt. To a Mexican or Latin American, however, Spain is efficient, honest and friendly.

Because things like Residencia requirements, work permits, health services, social welfare and telecommunications etc. can change fom year to year, I found the following website particularly detailed and strongly recommend it for up-to-date information. Using Google, type in "British Consulate Alicante" and you will find a website headed "British Embassies and Consulates in Spain". The list of topics of interest for both tourists and residents is on the righthand side of the page.

BUREAUCRACY AND RED TAPE

It is a fact that for many years, Spain was very 'backward' in comparison to the rest of Europe. Spaniards were content to run things on a very casual basis, not concerned that it might take a whole day to get a specific permit simply because it necessitated travelling all over the town or city to collect all the bits of paper and all the signatures required. Tremendous progress has been made in the last few years and efforts to streamline administrative offices have overcome some of the worst confusions and delays. But even to this day, your patience will be tried to the utmost on occasion, and you must learn to remain calm and reasonable under quite severe stress.

Visits to official departments, notaries, etc. can involve much time and patience, not just for foreigners but also for Spaniards. They accept it as normal and often with humour. As one Spaniard once said, "The delays are deliberate. This way one makes friends because you talk to people while you wait."

The tourist will have little contact with officialdom. The potential worker or resident will have much. Problems can be overcome to a certain extent by paying a middle man to take care of the negotiations. To do it yourself though is more fun and puts you in touch with helpful and friendly, if occasionally frustrating, Spaniards.

Spain, like other European countries, is in a state of change as it becomes fully integrated into the European Union. Rules for people from the EU and for those from outside are different. Changes take time to work through and this can lead to problems; offices in different areas may be working to different instructions.

Gestoria
The Spanish *gestor* is someone who can carry out most of the standard bureaucratic procedures on your behalf. He is not a

lawyer but he knows the intricacies of Spanish bureaucracy and is therefore able to do all the necessary paper work in connection with matters such as *residencias*, house rates, wealth and income taxes, and produce a result for a fee. You can, of course, deal with these matters yourself but are likely to find the paperwork not only confusing, but time-consuming and possibly even stressful!

RESIDENCE REQUIREMENTS

Living in Spain does not necessarily mean you need to apply for permanent residence. The first thing to decide is whether you actually want to become a resident as this will dictate how you proceed. Foreigners coming to retire rather than to work quite often choose to remain permanent tourists, for a variety of reasons.

Residence Permits (Residencias)

Residence permits are identity documents (with your picture and fingerprint) which non-Spanish residents of Spain are required to carry. For non-European Union nationals, it is essential to obtain entry visas from your local Spanish embassy or consulate before leaving your home country. If you plan to work in Spain, this must be stated when you apply for your visa, otherwise you could end up with a valid visa that does not let you do what you actually had planned to do. Such a visa is only good for 90 days and you must apply for your *residencia* before it expires.

Nationals of European Union countries have a right to reside in Spain and no visa is required. However, if they intend to stay longer than three months, they are expected, the day after arriving, to begin the process of applying for a *residencia* permit.

EU nationals working in Spain are granted a 'Community Card' which normally lasts for five years, but non-workers need to renew it at two-yearly intervals.

The next step is to buy a *papel de pagos* at an *estanco* (state tobacconist) which you hand in with your application to the *Comisario de Policio* who will tell you what the fee is in your case. You will be given a *resguardo* (receipt) which you must

Necessary Documents

Other requirements may include the following but they can vary from district to district. You would be well advised to go to the *Extranjeros* (foreigners') department at the nearest office of the *Comisaria de la Policia Nacional* (National Police) and check out the list of requirements which is normally posted there.

However, the first step for anyone planning to reside in Spain is the acquisition of a NIE Number (Numero de Identifacion Extranjero) because without one, you would be unable to conduct any kind of transaction, such as opening a bank account or buying a car. Don't forget to have:

- NIE number
- Original and photocopy of your passport
- Proof that you have somewhere to live, for example a document called an *escritura*.
- At least three passport-size colour photographs

guard carefully until you are told where and on what date to present yourself for fingerprinting before your application for *residencia* can be granted.

In some instances, you may also have to prove a monthly income of a certain number of euros, depending on your location. These amounts can vary considerably so choose your area carefully to make sure you can afford this requirement. Even so, there is no guarantee that the monthly requirement will remain the same.

All documents are required in duplicate, accompanied by three photographs. It is therefore worth having a set of photographs taken whenever you pass a photo booth (when you are neat and tidy) because you will soon be needing them if you plan to stay in Spain.

Recently, it has also become necessary for couples to provide a certificate of *Convivencia* obtained from the Ayuntamiento Town Hall and completed during a police visit to your home to prove that you are living with the person you claim to be with.

ME....WORK?!?

TRIGG.

WORK PERMITS

If you are coming from outide the EU and plan to reside and work in Spain, you have to apply for a work permit. This can take time to process, depending on the sort of work you plan to do. The Ministry Of Labour has to be satisfied that you are not displacing or depriving a Spanish worker and the police have to be assured that you have no criminal record.

Self-employment

If you want to be self-employed, it may take you up to six months or more to get your project approved and licensed. However, you still need a work permit and other documents to work in your own business. *(See Chapter 9 for details.)*

FOREIGN EXCHANGE REGULATIONS

Before 1992, stringent foreign exchange restrictions existed but now there are only two requirements in connection with foreign exchange and both are intended to prevent laundering of 'illegal currency' (drug money, for example).

As no border customs control exists now, the completion of the following forms allows Spanish banks to monitor transfers of large sums of cash and to control transactions that do not comply with the currency regulations.

- (a) Anyone bringing in cash in any currency valued at over 6,010 euros for crediting to a bank account in Spain must obtain and complete document B1.

- (b) Cash transactions, including cheques made out to *Al Portador* (cash), between residents and non-residents in Spain (for example residents selling property to non-residents) require the completion of document B3. These measures are required so that if it is then desired to export the proceeds from the transaction or to transfer large amounts from your account, proof is available to show where the money actually originated.

Opening A Bank Account

Opening an account is a relatively simple process. The bank of your choice will have a form for you to complete, requesting various references, your NIE number and photocopies of your passport or *residencia*. A *cuenta corriente* (current account) entitles you to a cheque book. Except in summer, banks are normally open on Saturday afternoons.

SALE AND PURCHASE OF PROPERTIES

There are no longer any restrictions regarding the purchase and sale of properties in Spain but both residents and non-residents are liable to capital gains when they sell. A non-resident will be charged a maximum capital gains tax of 35 per cent if he has owned his property for less than two years. The tax becomes less the longer the property has been owned.

Urbanisations

If the property you are considering is part of an urbanisation, there is less risk of finding you have no right of way over the only access road to your piece of land. Some developers, however, having sold all the houses on a particular urbanisation, may conveniently 'forget' to complete the urbanisation requirements. Roads may not be properly

Property prices in Spain are low compared with many other countries in Europe. Many foreigners own charming whitewashed villas on the *costas*.

surfaced, or street lighting required by the municipality may not be installed, or perhaps your electricity has not been properly connected. There are endless possibilities along these lines and this is where the real test comes. Trying to get such matters finalised can involve a lot of running around.

Buyers of property in the Valencian autonomous community should be aware that under the Valencian Government's *Ley Reguladora de la Actividad Urbanistica* of 1994, all land may be converted for property development unless it has been deemed non-urbanisable on historical, cultural or ecological grounds.

This means that even *suelo rustico* (rural land) may be re-designated as fit for property development if the town hall approves a developer's plans for such a change. It is therefore important, when buying a property, to check future development plans at the

A Helping Hand

There are usually property owner's associations in areas where most foreigners settle. These specialise in assisting foreign property owners. Some of them even publish monthly bulletins to keep foreigners updated on any changes in Spanish laws which might affect them personally.

town hall, and a prospective purchaser is advised to seek professional advice from a reliable lawyer.

Multas

A *multa* is a fine. Some associations notify their members if they are named by the *Ayuntamiento* or another authority for being behind on payments. They also publish the names of non-members in their bulletins because frequently the house or debt is in the name of a relative with a different surname. This is known as the 'early warning system' and has, on occasion, saved the owner from fines for non-payment of a tax about which he knew nothing. If he happens to owe a large amount in unpaid taxes, his property could be put up for public auction to raise the funds for the outstanding debt. Should he be out of Spain at the time, this could occur without his knowledge. Owners have been known to return to find they no longer own property.

ELECTRICITY

Iberdrola, the national electricity company, now has a website (http://www.ciberdrola.com) which can provide the user with a wealth of detailed information.

Electricity failures are much rarer nowadays except when there have been particularly savage storms or unusual

amounts of snow. In recent years, electricity supply lines are being laid underground but it is still quite common to see villages festooned with electricity lines from house to house and street to street. One wonders how more people aren't electrocuted!

If you find your electricity going off suddenly, first check your main fuse. If all your fuses are in order, the next step is to ring the electricity people. They may tell you that they are laying new lines and not to worry, your supply will be restored in an hour or two, or they may tell you that your bill hasn't been paid. This is normally taken care of by your bank, but mistakes can and do occur.

Free Electricity!

One couple we know were comfortably installed in their new house, delighted with the seeming ease with which they had 'settled in Spain'. Suddenly, they were surprised to find that their electricity supply seemed to be free of charge. They did not worry about it until the day they were warned it was about to be cut off. It was only then that they found out that their small urbanisation, a total of seven houses, had only one electricity metre in the name of the developer. He had been paying the account until he suddenly ran out of money.

Their immediate thought was: 'Fine, we can get our own meter.' But when they applied to the electricity board, they were informed that no meters could be allocated to individual houses on the estate until roads and street lights, etc. were completed to the standard required by the municipality. Since the developer was bankrupt, how would this be done? Of the seven houses, only three were more or less permanently occupied. The owners of the remaining four only used them for brief periods in summer and were therefore unlikely to want to fork out vast sums to finish roadworks and install street lamps.

The short-term solution involved the three resident owners raising sufficient funds between them to pay the outstanding electricity account, which at least allowed them a period of approximately two months to figure a way out of their dilemma before the next bill was due. Frequent meetings between the resident owners took place, including conferences with the local mayor, municipal architect and legal advisers. Numerous letters were exchanged with non-resident owners informing them of actions being taken and requesting their share of contributions for payment of bills. All this eventually led to the discovery that no progress could be made unless the seven owners of the urbanisation teamed up and created a 'community', for which purpose a special law exists to govern how owners should conduct their joint affairs.

In some parts of Spain, electricity wires can still be seen hanging above village streets.

Ley de Propriedad Horizontal

The law of horizontal property applies anywhere where owners possess things in common, such as pools, tennis courts, roads or sewage disposal systems, and in this particular instance... the electricity meter!

Electrical Appliances

The electric current in Spain is 220 volts and the plugs take two round prongs. So, if you are coming from the United States, you will need an adaptor even for small appliances such as hair dryers. I once thoughtlessly plugged in a hair dryer bought in the States and left it on my dressing table for a short period. I came back to find that my hair dryer had melted!

WATER SUPPLY

Before the influx of foreigners buying properties and building swimming pools, the water supply along the coastal areas was adequate, except in the deserts around Murcia and Almeria. Then came the drought years when the rainfall was less than normal. Houses which had been built without *depositos* (holding tanks) to store water faced problems. Water cuts were frequent and restrictions on water usage quite stringent. The water table in some areas dropped so low that sea-water penetrated the underground wells. Even if water came from the taps, it was often too salty to be used in cooking or for watering plants.

This situation was remedied by two years of adequate rainfall but, once again, a serious drought situation exists in the southern parts of Spain. The water in most areas is now of a sufficiently high quality for drinking and cooking, though many people still prefer to buy bottled water for personal consumption.

BASURAS

Nowadays, rubbish collecting systems exist in most areas. If the circuit of the rubbish lorries does not include your urbanisation or area, there are large skips placed at frequent intervals along the roads into which you can dump your household refuse. Because of the pollution caused by random dumping of rubbish, some municipalities actually print a pamphlet specifying the correct procedures to be followed. Care must be taken not to scatter rubbish indiscriminately around the skips. You might find yourself pounced on by a *basura* (rubbish) inspector lurking nearby, who will be watching carefully to ensure correct use is made of the skips.

Recycling

These days most areas provide bins of different shapes and colours for recycling:

- **Household and Organic Rubbish but NOT GARDEN WASTE:** vegetables, fruit and food remains.
- **Packaging**: tins, tetrabriks, aluminium paper, plastic bags and bottles.
- **Glass**: all glass containers (without caps). NOT CHINA OR CERAMICS.
- **Paper and Cardboard**: all cardboard, newspapers and magazines.
- **Clothing**: clothes and shoes.
- For **Larger Items** such as furniture and domestic appliances, residents usually call a telephone number which is supplied and are told of the appropriate procedure.

Street Cleaning

If you are accustomed to the streets being cleaned by municipal workmen, it may come as a shock to you that, in some villages and small towns, you are expected to personally keep the pavement, gutter and road outside your house clean. The proper way to do this is by sprinkling water from a bucket (a hard-to-master technique) or with a hose. In Spanish households, this task is still largely performed by women.

TAXES

Residents are charged income tax on world income. They may also have to pay local taxes and sometimes a wealth tax as well. Property-owning tourists should pay the local property tax, the wealth tax and income tax on the letting value of their property in Spain, even if the property is never rented out. You are deemed a fiscal resident if you remain in Spain for more than 183 days in a calendar year. You do not need to submit income tax returns if your yearly income does not exceed a certain amount. This amount depends on where the income arises, whether it is a pension, etc. and can vary from year to year. It is therefore recommended that you seek advice from a *gestor* in April/May every year when any new tax regulations may come into force.

EDUCATION

A 1970 Act made it compulsory for children to attend school between the ages of six and 14, and this basic schooling is available at no cost. After completing basic education, the pupils are faced with a choice of either three years of further academic study, plus another one-year course intended to prepare them for university, or two-year courses providing a general introduction to professions such as clerical work

IT'S FOR MY OWN SAFETY

Nursery children going for a walk are often seen strung together by a rope, which keeps them from straying.

or hairdressing, which can be followed by another two-year course offering specialised vocational training.

From being one of the poorest nations in respect of schools and universities, Spanish standards can now be favourably compared with the rest of Europe.

Kindergartens

Most parents send their children to nursery schools either to ensure that they get a good start, or simply to get the children out of the way during the day. It is a common sight in some of the larger cities to see a crocodile of small children tethered together with a rope being led along by an adult. These are not miniature criminals being led off to jail; merely nursery schoolchildren being taken for a walk by their teacher—tethered together for their own protection!

Schools

Apart from state-run schools, which accept foreign students, there are also a number of foreign schools available. Completely English or American ones are run on exactly the same systems as schools in England and America, with the same targets, and the standards are usually very good.

Some parents prefer to send their children to English/Spanish bilingual schools. Here, Spanish language classes are usually very demanding whereas the English classes are geared towards second language learners. It isn't easy to find schools which prepare children equally well in both languages. Also, Spanish standards for mathematics and science are considerably higher than in the United States, which could make things difficult for a new student.

Use the Internet

The website http://www.spanishpropertyworld.com is a very informative site which not only provides complete listings of available properties all over Spain, but also advice about European schools which are jointly controlled by governments of Member States of the European Union.

The website also provides information on Nursery, Primary and Secondary education in English, French, Spanish and German. In addition, you can find out about International Schools offering courses for the International General Certificate of Secondary Education (IGCSE), the equivalent to the UK GCSE, or the International Baccalaureate organisation which offers three programmes to a wide variety of schools throughout Spain.

When it comes to lunch, only some schools offer this facility to students. If you live near the school, your children can come home for lunch. Otherwise they can bring packed lunches. There is no hard and fast rule.

'Bedtime!'

This word creates problems for foreign parents who feel their children of school-going age should retire to bed at a reasonable time in order to be fresh and alert for lessons the following day. "It's hard to get kids to bed at a decent hour," says a Canadian, "when all the neighbourhood children are still out with their bikes and skateboards. School-going children are often out with their friends until 9:00 pm or 10:00 pm during term-time, and until 11:00 pm or 12:00 am during the summer!'

Universities

The number of university students more than tripled in the 1960s. By the early 1970s, nearly a quarter of a million students attended one of the 30-or-so universities in Spain, a few of which are run by the Church and one by Opus Dei.

The two biggest, the Complutense in Madrid and the Central in Barcelona, are responsible for more than half the total number of students. Spanish universities make a clear distinction between academic and practical studies. Conventional faculties and colleges offer traditional disciplines which may take five or six years. University schools offer courses for training as teachers, nurses and the like. The universities have more than half a million undergraduates and graduate employment has been a problem since the mid-1970s.

SHOPPING

Cities and towns have department stores, boutiques and supermarkets where you can find the same items as elsewhere in Europe. If you live in a village, of course, you may have some difficulty getting smart clothes, furnishings and luxury goods.

In small towns and villages, most shops have no name or sign—everyone knows what they sell and where they are. The shopping is mostly left to women, although men may go to the baker's for bread. Women who are not working make shopping a daily affair, a social occasion, with separate trips to the baker, supermarket, bank or butcher. Loyalty—often family loyalty—means patronising the same shops, except on the days when the weekly open-air market is on.

Food shopping is a real treat in Spain. The range and quality of seasonal fruit and vegetables is excellent; dairy products tend to be more expensive than elsewhere in Europe; chickens are first class; and although Spanish butchers chop up meat in ways which you may find odd, once you figure it out, you can buy whatever you want.

Metric System

It is useful to remember that Spaniards are unlikely to understand pounds and ounces. Should your request for 'a pound of potatoes' draw a blank look, rather than repeating your request, you could try pointing at the potatoes and

In a covered market, a butcher's stall advertises the sale of bull meat after a bullfight.

asking for "*Medio kilo, por favor*" ("Half a kilo, please"). But these days, many shopkeepers understand English.

In fact, if you work on the basis that half a kilo is equivalent to one pound, you will be getting approximately the amount you desire. If you don't know the Spanish name for what you want, pointing at it is quite acceptable.

Covered Markets

Large or small depending on the size of the town or village, these markets are made up of rows of stalls, some selling fruit and vegetables, others chickens and eggs, or meats and sausages and some, a variety of grocery items including cheese and other delicacies. One stall will be devoted to bread and cakes of all kinds, another may display containers full of pickled vegetables and huge quantities of differently flavoured olives. Covered markets are still popular with local people even though they are, in fact, no cheaper than the big supermarkets which have sprung up everywhere.

Open-air Markets

Each village has an open-air market once a week on a specific day when stalls are put up in neat rows offering the widest imaginable range of goods for sale. The vegetable stalls are a joy to behold, with their piles of red and green pimientos, stacks of huge, shiny purple aubergines, mountains of enormous white cauliflowers and boxes of luscious strawberries in season. Although salad items are available throughout the year, some vegetables are seasonal. If you buy 'seasonally' you will not be disappointed; the prices are lower. In general, locally grown vegetables and fruits are cheaper than in northern Europe.

In addition to food, open-air markets usually have rows of stalls displaying clothing, shoes, handbags and belts, as well as tourist items. But don't think you will be getting bargain prices. Check out prices in local shops offering similar goods and you will find the market prices are sometimes even higher, specially designed for the unwary tourist who's in a hurry.

The bakery is a regular stop for full-time housewives on their shopping rounds.

Rastros

The equivalent of 'flea markets', *rastros* are set up on specific days in different locations, details of which are usually advertised in local newspapers. They are a popular way to spend a few hours searching for the odd bargains, which occasionally can be found to the delight of the purchaser. All kinds of items are offered for sale from junk to antiques to jewellery. Some *rastros* also attract stamp dealers and coin collectors.

Beware!

Pickpockets and bag-snatchers have a field day amongst the massed shoppers at open-air markets. If possible, you should leave your handbag safely locked up at home, and clutch your purse or wallet tightly in your hand.

Haggling

You will gain no advantage by bargaining with a stall holder over the price of potatoes or carrots because standard products in daily demand are sold at standard prices. However, if you are looking for items such as watches or small radios, you might succeed in lowering the asking price. Also, the carpet-sellers from North Africa and the gypsy women selling lace tablecloths may be willing to haggle.

Don't haggle just for the fun of it as stall holders will resent your wasting their time. Do haggle if you know the price you are prepared to pay and are keen to acquire the item in question. When the stall holder tells you his price, you make your offer. What this may be depends on what you are prepared to pay. You could start with a quarter of his asking price, with the intention of working up to half, or start with half and stick to it. When the final price is agreed, try to hand over the right amount of euros because if you give the seller a large note for a small amount, he may decide that you can afford to pay more and tell you that you misunderstood the agreed price.

Hypermarkets

Most sizeable towns will have one of these enormous supermarkets where virtually everything under the sun is available. Here you will find the prices fractionally lower than in the smaller supermarkets. Some hypermarkets will even offer to repay *autopista* (motorway) fees to encourage customers from outlying areas.

You can try your bargaining skills at a gypsy stall. But do not haggle if you have no intention of buying.

Department Stores

If you don't speak Spanish, department stores would probably be the easiest way for you to do your shopping. El Corte Ingles is a chain with a wide range of good quality items. Its main competitor is Galerias Preciados which can also be found in most of the major towns.

Queues

Spaniards do not like forming queues. Lining up one behind the other seems to go against their individualistic character. Consequently watch out for people trying to cut in. This *yo primero* (me first) trait also applies to driving in the city or on open roads, a case of 'survival of the fittest'.

Even though Spaniards do not form neat and orderly queues, they instinctively manage to keep good order and take their turn at the right time. Market stall holders will refuse to serve a 'queue jumper' and simply ignore him until they are ready to serve him. Nowadays, there is a system of numbers at some of the supermarket counters, particularly the meat and fish counters. You take a number from a roll fixed on the counter and wait for it to be called. If there are lots of numbers ahead of your own, this leaves you free to carry on with other shopping until your turn draws near. But make sure you are available when your number is called. Otherwise you will be made to draw a new number and wait all over again.

Shopping Hours

Open-air markets start early and pack up just after 1:00 pm; covered markets follow the Spanish custom and are closed during the afternoon hours of *siesta*, but they do stay open until quite late in the evening, some even as late as 9:00 pm. Some supermarkets also observe the *siesta* and usually re-open only around 4:30 pm, although the family-run ones tend to have their own opening hours. As small green grocer shops in villages tend to be both owned and run by a family, the hours kept can vary considerably. However, most of them would observe the *siesta*. Hypermarkets and department stores remain open all day.

HEALTH SERVICES

Most of the embassies have websites nowadays which provide comprehensive sections covering medical insurance and treatment in Spain. Particularly informative is http://www.ukinspain.com.

Insalud, the National Health Institute, provides health care, free of charge, to approximately 98.9 per cent of the population. Statistics show that the population is long-lived (76.18 years for men, the highest in the EU, and 83.08 years for women, the second highest in the EU); and is relatively healthy, considering factors such as climate, food and way of life. Spain has the fewest deaths from cancer in the EU.

Nowadays, most foreigners have nothing but praise for the health services. Ambulances arrive promptly and patients are whisked to the appropriate hospital or clinic for treatment. For national health services, you have to register with a specific doctor.

Home Visits

Minor ailments can be treated by private doctors, either at their clinic or, if necessary, at home. Spanish doctors are still quite prepared to pay daily calls on patients in their homes, if necessary.

Hospitals

Spanish hospitals usually provide an extra bed in the patient's room. This is for the family member who accompanies the patient to hospital. Qualified nurses handle the skilled work and the patient's family is expected to attend to the patient's comfort. Nowadays, some of the more modern hospitals or clinics in the larger cities no longer expect a patient's family to provide this service, but many still have the extra bed in case it is desired. Most hospitals are well staffed and the standard of specialised treatment is high.

Social Welfare

Reciprocal arrangements have existed since 1971 between most of the European countries, and if a foreigner is entitled to free medical and dental care in his own country, he can usually obtain it just as easily in Spain. Before coming to Spain, you should apply for the new European Health Insurance Card (EHIC). Application forms are available at post offices.

Friends (retired on the Costa Blanca) say that the service is excellent, the doctors usually understand foreign languages and the equipment in the hospitals and dental clinics is very modern. Friends working in Madrid, on the other hand, complain that emergency services are depressing and often overcrowded, and that there could be months of waiting for X-rays, operations, etc. in the social security system. They consider it mandatory to have a separate insurance to cover most medical care.

Public Health

'Don't drink water from the tap or eat uncooked vegetables' used to be good advice when travelling about in Spain and people who did not heed it often succumbed to violent attacks of 'Spanish tummy' which was more than just the result of a change of climate and diet. After the tragedy of what was called the 'toxic syndrome' in the early 1980s which claimed over 300 lives, food inspection and regulations controlling standards of hygiene in bars and restaurants were tightened and one no longer needs to avoid salads when dining out.

Now that Spain is a member of the European Union, all food and drink has to be labelled in accordance with EU standards, clearly showing expiry dates, etc.

Chemists

Each chemist shop in Spain is owned and operated by a qualified chemist who is not permitted to own more than one shop. All the chemist shops in a certain area take turns to remain open as a *farmacia de guardia* for 24 hours a day, and a small notice on the door of a closed chemist will tell you which one is open on that particular day or night.

Chemists stock medicines, medical products, hair sprays, cosmetics and soaps. Also available are baby foods, which

Buying medicine in a *farmacia* is easy as the chemist is usually helpful and friendly. You usually do not need a prescription to get most types of different medicines.

are also sold in supermarkets and hypermarkets. Medicines purchased outside Spain can probably be replaced by a Spanish equivalent, but you should be able to give the chemist the brand and manufacturer's name and, most importantly, the formula. If the chemist does not have the required medicine in stock, he can usually get it quite quickly by phoning wholesalers in the vicinity.

Spanish 'Cure-alls'

Spaniards believe you will get sick if you don't wear your slippers or if you stay in a draught or get your 'kidneys' cold. When you are sick, their 'cure-all' is either hot milk laced with brandy and honey or warm lemon juice with honey. These are whole-heartedly recommended... they taste wonderful regardless of how effective they may be!

Qualified chemists often offer medical advice and if you know which medicine is effective for your particular ailment, you will be able to purchase it over the counter from a chemist without incurring the expense of a doctor's visit beforehand.

Most foreigners are amazed at how easy it is to get medicine (which would require a doctor's prescription elsewhere) without any prescription from a chemist in Spain, and usually at a fraction of the cost. However, inhalers for asthmatic patients DO require a doctor's prescription.

DRUGS

Spain's proximity to North Africa and links with Latin America make drugs like marijuana and cocaine comparatively easy to come by. A survey carried out some years ago on army conscripts showed that 60 per cent had experimented with drugs by the time they were enlisted in their late teens. Today, it is difficult to find a young Spaniard who has not, at one time or another, smoked pot. The fact that it is not a punishable crime to be in possession of small amounts of marijuana for 'personal use' is certainly no deterrent. However, the real problem is in the trafficking of hard drugs, which sprang up after Franco's death.

Madrid's airport, although it possesses some of the most sophisticated drug detection equipment in the world, still sees 60 per cent of all South American cocaine passing through it, not only for the Spanish market but also for the rest of

Europe. Many unemployed youths from all over Europe flock to the Balearics for a quick and cheap 'fix'.

VOLUNTARY HELP GROUPS

Independent help groups operate in several Costa Blanca municipalities and similar groups will be found in other parts of Spain. Volunteers will provide neighbourly assistance in cases of emergency. During rehabilitation periods after hospitalisation, they will visit the elderly who may be housebound and, if necessary, do the grocery shopping.

Red Cross Posts

You will find these posts at intervals along the main motorways and usually in the larger villages as well. They are staffed and equipped to deal with accidents on the spot.

Instead of doing their military service (250,000 young men are conscripted into the army every year for a minimum service of 12 months), young men can opt for a longer period of service with the Red Cross. After six weeks' training, the 'volunteer' is presented with a pair of socks and a pair of underpants! The rest of his clothing, plus the cost of food and accommodation, is the responsibility of fund-raisers in the town where he serves. However, due to recent changes in the

conditions for military service, the Red Cross is experiencing a shortage of staff, especially ambulance drivers.

Much of the Red Cross' funds are raised by 'flag' sales to motorists waiting at traffic lights or in summer traffic jams; but this can be hazardous. Some towns prefer to provide the necessary money from public funds after boys were involved in accidents whilst attempting to sell flags at crossroads.

INSURANCE
It is advisable to have your house and contents insured and this is easily done through any one of the many insurance companies, either Spanish or foreign, operating in the towns and cities. They will probably send a representative to inspect your property and advise you about security measures. If you own paintings and/or other objects of value, it is best to itemise them or even have photographs available so that they can be more easily traced should they be stolen. Your car must carry at least third party insurance and this can also be easily arranged locally.

Taking up life or medical insurance is a question of personal choice. If you have reciprocal national health benefits, registering with a doctor in your community will entitle you to free medical treatment and medicine. However, in some instances, additional medical insurance appears to be desirable, particularly in the larger, more crowded cities where private treatment would doubtless ensure speedier attention in times of emergency.

TRANSPORTATION
City Transport
You can get around Spain in a number of ways, including trains, buses and even bicycles, should you so desire.

Madrid has an excellent underground system which is quick, frequent and cheap no matter how far you travel. Even cheaper is the 10-ride ticket called *billet de diez* which is accepted by the automatic turnstiles.

City buses run from 6:00 am until midnight. This is for both the red full-sized buses and the yellow microbuses which are somewhat more comfortable. Taxi stands are numerous and taxis are easily hailed in the street—except when it rains!

In Barcelona, the underground is the fastest and cheapest way of getting around, as well as the easiest to use. Although a flat rate is charged no matter how far you travel, buying a *Targeta T2* is even more economical. Good for ten rides, it is valid for the underground, *tramvia blau*, funicular and central *ferrocariles* (railway). By buying a *Targeta T1*, you will also be entitled to travel on buses.

Beyond The Call Of Duty

Most traffic policemen are very helpful. We were once thoroughly lost in Madrid during rush hour and stopped by the side of a policeman controlling traffic at a busy intersection. We knew that the address we were looking for was nearby but explained that we had been unsuccessful in our search, could he tell us how to get there?

He climbed off his pedestal and scrambled into the back seat of our car and proceeded to direct us to our destination... leaving the busy intersection to its own fate! We offered him a few *pesetas* when he got out to pay for a taxi to take him back to his post, but he refused with a smile, stopped the first car that passed, climbed in and cheerfully told the driver to deposit him back at his busy intersection!

Trains

In general, RENFE, the government-run railroad, is below par by European standards. The first high-speed train between Madrid and Seville made its debut just in time for the 1992 Expo. Long-distance runs are mostly made at night and can be very slow. Train travel, however, is probably the most economical method of getting around Spain. First- and second-class seats are reasonably priced but both food and drink in the dining cars and bars are over-priced and more often than not, uninspiring.

If you are an *aficionado* (fan) of antique trains, RENFE operates the luxurious turn-of-the-century Al-Andalus Express which makes two-day and three-day trips for sightseeing purposes in Cordoba, Granada and Seville, and also runs from Pamplona to Santiago de Compostela along the Way of St James during the summer. Kings and queens used to travel on these trains which have been beautifully restored down to the smallest detail. Even the sleeping compartments complete the mood of old-time elegance.

Buses

Private companies run the bus services which can range from knee-crunching basic to luxurious. Fares tend to be lower than for rail travel and you can be fairly sure to find buses to take you to destinations not serviced by trains. Eurolines/National Express consortium has regular coach services from London to more than 45 destinations in Spain. These journeys take about 26 hours to Barcelona or 32 hours to Madrid and run twice a week throughout the year. Fares are reasonable and the coaches provide TV entertainment and toilet facilities. There are also coach services linking the various cities.

Rules Have Their Own Set Of Rules

The authorities have been known to turn a blind eye on law infringement for a period of time if they believe they have a good reason to do so. For example, a yacht owner, having got into debt, decided to make some money by chartering his boat. This is strictly not allowed, but no one seemed to mind nor was any attempt made to stop him. Then one day, the police pounced on him. When he asked why, he was told, "You have made enough money to pay all your debts so now you must stop breaking the law."

Bicycles

Bicycle trips require careful planning because of the mountainous terrain and crowded roads you are likely to encounter. The *Route of El Cid* prepared by the Tourist Office is a 20-day cycling tour which can be a great help should you wish to pedal from Burgos to Valencia.

Cyclists have to be careful on the road, but cycling is a very popular sport in Spain and a mode of transport. Other road users are unusually wary of cyclists, automatically slowing down when overtaking.

Cars

While you are applying for *residencia*, you will be permitted to import a foreign registered car without paying customs duty. As soon as your *residencia* is granted, your car will have to be replaced with a Spanish-registered one. However, you do not need to do so if you have obtained a *prorogacion* (special exemption) before you applied for *residencia*. It may be granted for one year on payment of a proportion of import duty, and this can be repeated for four consecutive years, after which you either complete the importation or remove the car from Spain. As the customs valuation of your car may be higher than you anticipate, it is wise to get a quotation before committing yourself.

Choose The Right Make

Although a large American or European make of car may be more comfortable for long-distance travel, you would do well to remember that many of the older towns and villages have very narrow streets which hamper the use of such cars because their wide frames make them difficult to manoeuvre.

In the summer season, cars travel at a snail's pace, nose to tail along the coast. *Autopistas* operated on a toll system tend to be less congested. Most places have traffic police to deal with congestions and to make sure that parking restrictions are adhered to. Until recently, Spaniards were in the habit of leaving their cars wherever convenient, often double or even triple parked. In Madrid, when the Spanish equivalent of English clamps was first introduced, it almost caused a major riot. People demonstrated and many who attacked the clamps with sledgehammers were taken to court.

Perhaps careless parking by tourists merely reflects their desire to follow the Spanish example but increased surveillance by local traffic police and designation of properly marked and controlled parking areas have improved the general circulation of traffic.

Car Rentals

Many car rental agencies exist and, in most places, as long as you are over 21 years of age, possess a valid EU driving licence and a current credit card, renting a car is a very simple matter and there is usually a wide range of vehicle types for you to choose from.

Many villages in Spain date from the Middle Ages. Their narrow streets make large cars from America or Europe very impractical.

Foreign Registered Cars

A tourist can use a foreign registered car for six months per calendar year in Spain. This goes up to nine if you are from 'overseas', i.e. USA, Australia or the Far East, etc .

If you want to leave your car in Spain but only spend six months of the year there, you can get the customs to 'seal' your car during your absence. However, the *prorogacion* procedure is also available and extensions can be obtained by importing on a temporary basis, as mentioned above.

Car Papers

You are required by law to have 'car papers' with you whether you are driving a Spanish or foreign registered car, so that these can be presented to the police upon request. These papers include the registration book, insurance certificate, your own driving licence and personal identification papers. If you have a *residencia*, it is unlikely that your passport will be required. If you are caught driving without these papers, you might find yourself having to pay a hefty fine.

Driving Licence

As a resident with a Spanish registered car, you will eventually have to acquire a Spanish driving licence. To get one, you must apply to the Jefatura de Trafico in any provincial capital by presenting your licence and paying a small fee. After quite a lot of paperwork and possibly an interval of some hours, a Spanish licence will be handed to you, but your original one will be retained. However, as a Spanish resident, you can use the Spanish licence anywhere in the EU.

Blowing Whistles

Policemen in other countries usually refrain from blowing their whistles except in moments of urgency when trying to prevent a crime. In Spain, all traffic police are equipped with whistles which they blow continuously, making it very difficult at times to work out what they are trying to achieve. Are you meant to stop? Are you meant to go on? You must watch the policeman carefully to find out his intention, which is more easily identified by his hand or arm movements.

Visitors are often captivated by the charming streets of San Sebastian, Basque Country, in northern Spain.

Girls in traditional dress in Andalusia. Most women wear conventional clothing on a daily basis, reserving their attractive mutli-tiered dresses for festivals and other special occasions.

Madrid by dusk is a visual feast as well-designed lighting highlight the fine architectural details of structures such as the Metropolis Building.

Restaurant in Plaza Major in Madrid specialises in *tapas* (above) while
paella (below) is another local favourite.
Opposite: Al-fresco dining is a popular option with both locals and visitors
when the weather is pleasant.

Parts of Spain are very mountainous and homes such as these in Caseras offer views of the Andalucian hills.

Flashing Headlights

You may also find yourself confused by flashing headlights. In England, if a car flashes its headlights at you, you can safely assume that the driver is indicating 'Go ahead'. Don't imagine this is true in Spain where flashing headlights can mean just about anything, most frequently 'Get out of my way!'

Sometimes a car coming towards you from the opposite direction will flash its headlights, trying to warn you that there is a traffic patrol ahead, or that there has been an accident. Whatever it may mean, if this happens you should always slow down.

Taking the Wheel

When in Spain, you might find it necessary to drive the way Spaniards do. They tend to be aggressive drivers, cutting in and out of lanes, paying little attention to traffic rules or the needs of other roadusers. When you approach that amber light and your instinct tells you to apply your brakes, first look in your rear-view mirror to make sure you do not have a Spaniard close behind you. You might find yourself being rear-ended unless you step on the accelerator and zoom right on through! In fact, it is well to drive with greater care than usual, keeping an eye on your rear-view mirror, in order to avoid unnecessary repairs. If you happen to get involved in an accident with a Spaniard, chances are that you will be found 'guilty' and fined, no matter who actually caused the accident.

Autopistas (Motorways)

Motorways in Spain are extensive, well-surfaced but expensive, unlike those of England and

Modern-day Highwaymen

Tourists, in particular, fall victim to modern-day highwaymen. They are unaware that accomplices telephone their travel plans ahead to modern-day highwaymen who pay handsomely for descriptions of choice victims and their belongings. Tourists naively accept advice from a friendly stranger who may recommend a particularly picturesque and traffic-free route, giving the bandits the opportunity to carry out their ambush. Another favourite technique is to drive alongside a foreign car and yell that a tyre is flat. When the unsuspecting holiday-maker pulls over, the gang pounces. More than 1,000 vehicles fall victim to such bandits every year in Spain.

Autopistas are generally well-maintained and the fastest way to move from one town to another. However, they are expensive.

Germany which are free. The rates go up pretty regularly each year. The speed limit in Spain is 120 kmph (74 mph), but you will find many drivers exceeding this limit. Watch out for road patrols as fines for speeding are instantaneous and can be heavy.

Rest Areas

As in other countries, you are not allowed to stop on the *autopistas* but, every now and then, there are areas where you can get petrol and buy a wide range of refreshments. Some places have proper restaurants that serve standard meals; almost all will display a selection of *tapas* at the counter. Apart from a full range of soft drinks, you may be surprised to find you can buy beer and wine just as easily, even though drink-driving

Driving Tips

To drive in Spain you need a valid driving licence and be over 18 years old. Drivers should carry a first aid kit, spare light bulbs, a warning triangle and two reflective jackets for use in the event of either accidents or breakdowns.

offences are not treated lightly! However, it is wise not to leave your car unattended. Windows are frequently smashed and anything left lying on the seats removed. Also, beware of people asking advice about which route to follow. They may produce a map and make you peer at it closely. Whilst you are thus distracted, an accomplice will snatch whatever is handy and run off.

National Roads

The network of national roads is well maintained but the heavy lorry traffic can slow you down tremendously. Speed limits on these roads are 100 kmph (62 mph) on roads with hard shoulders on both sides, or 90 kmph (56 mph) on roads in open country.

Petrol

Petrol stations are now plentiful throughout Spain and, as prices are government-controlled, they are the same everywhere you go. Most of the stations offer regular, super and unleaded petrol as well as diesel. Credit cards are frequently accepted, particularly along main routes.

Road Patrols

Guardias on motorcycles (nicknamed 'heavenly twins' because they hunt in pairs) patrol the roads constantly. One is usually a trained mechanic and the other a first-aider so there are times when their arrival is welcome. On the other hand, if they catch you breaking the speed limit or crossing a double white line, they are permitted to stop and fine you on the spot, allowing you a 20 per cent discount if you pay your fine in cash! Offering them bribes is a waste of time.

As already mentioned, you are supposed to carry your car papers, driving licence and identification at all times.

Zebra Crossings

Rather than ensuring a safe crossing for pedestrians, these can be extremely hazardous and you are advised to be particularly careful when crossing roads. Recently, three elderly Spanish women were mown down by a car in

Benidorm whilst attempting to cross a dual carriage way at a point described as a 'pedestrian crossing'. The vehicle in this case was a Madrid-registered car driven by a Spaniard. Many drivers ignore the presence of pedestrians even if they are actually on the crossing, and accidents are frequent because some drivers also ignore speed restrictions. Some towns and villages provide traffic police at pedestrian crossings to ensure that pedestrians can cross safely and in some cities you will find the equivalent of 'WALK/DON'T WALK' lights on street corners. However, wherever you are, you really must approach even designated crossings with extreme caution.

LAW AND ORDER

Although the amount of crime committed in Spain is lower than in most of Europe, the police force in Spain is very large. The ratio is about one police officer for every 250 inhabitants. Urban areas are patrolled by three different sorts of forces. These are the Policia Municipal, the Policia Nacional and the Cuerpo Superior de Policia. The Guardia Civil is not considered part of the urban forces.

Staying within the law in Spain is easy as policemen are both friendly and helpful.

Policia Municipal

These are recruited locally and paid for by the town or city council concerned. They are responsible for traffic, parking and upholding local bylaws, and are found in any town with a population of over 5,000.

Policia Nacional

Uniformed forces employed by the government, organised on quasi-military lines, are found in towns of more than 20,000 inhabitants and highly industrialised centres. These have replaced the hated Policia Armada of Franco's era, and because of the change in their outlook and attitude, they are now quite popular with the public.

Cuerpo Superior de Policia

As the name implies, this is the most senior of the urban forces and consists of plain clothes officers who devise and administer the policing policies in each area.

Guardia Civil

The history of the Guardia Civil can be traced back to 1844 when the government set it up to combat banditry. Today, its main duties are to patrol the countryside, the motorways and frontiers, and act as customs officers. A few foreigners appear to fear the Guardias, but if you are a law-abiding citizen, you will find them extraordinarily civil and very helpful in times of need.

Staying within the Law

For some inexplicable reason, many foreigners coming to reside in Spain appear to believe that Spanish rules and regulations are not intended for them. They will build houses and pools without acquiring the necessary permits, they will ignore traffic regulations such as roundabouts, one-way streets and parking restrictions, and then act the injured party when they are suddenly hauled up and either taken to court or made to pay a fine. Pleading ignorance is no excuse because there is no reason to be ignorant of the law... anyone you talk to will be more than willing to give you advice. The important thing is to get the right advice and follow it.

Keeping within the law will ensure a cooperative attitude from the Spanish authorities. If you do the right thing, so will they. They are not out to hound you unless you take it upon yourself to ignore their laws.

MILITARY SERVICE

The death rate amongst Spanish youngsters doing their *mili* is ten times higher than for any other European national serviceman. Selection is made by a random process. The fate of the young men is decided by a nationally televised lottery when 365 balls inscribed with days and months are selected one by one.

It sometimes seems unfair that one youngster has to serve his country whilst a neighbour born on another day has the chance to continue his studies towards a lucrative career. Quite a few young soldiers attempt to commit suicide but less than a quarter are successful.

FIRE BRIGADE

Firefighters are kept busy in the summer in areas with pine forests. In most places, there are restrictions about when and where you can burn your garden rubbish and some areas insist that you advise the municipality and acquire their permission before lighting up. In any case, fires are strictly forbidden during the summer months when the countryside is particularly vulnerable to sparks which can set off dangerous forest fires.

TELECOMMUNICATIONS

Telefonica, the national telephone company, now has a website: http//: www.telefonicaonline.com (in Spanish) which provides a wealth of detailed information for subscribers. To get a line you must apply to Telefonica either by phone or by letter.

If you decide to have an ADSL line, look under "Internet" on the website recommended at the start of this chapter as there are choices to be made to ensure you get the best service.

There are also numerous shops selling different types of mobile phones throughout Spain.

The Postal System

The Spanish postal system is seldom praised for its speed and efficiency, particularly in the coastal areas where the influx of large numbers of foreigners has placed heavy demands on available postmen. The number of postmen in a certain area depends on the number of 'registered' residents in that area. If more foreigners registered with the local authorities, the situation would improve greatly.

Mail Deliveries

Letters are usually delivered once a day and to your door if your letter box is conveniently placed. Sometimes, in more rural areas, a number of boxes are grouped together at the end of a road so that the postman need make only one stop. A small parcel will be delivered to your door, but a larger one will be kept at the post office and you will receive a notice asking you to collect it. Proof of identity will be required.

A limited number of post office boxes are available in most post offices and these are allocated on a first-come-first-served basis. You may have to wait some time before one becomes available for you. However, letters addressed to you poste restante (called *Lista* in Spanish) can be collected when you produce your passport.

FOOD AND ENTERTAINING

CHAPTER 6

'Wine is a mocker, strong drink a brawler and
whoever is led astray by it is not wise.'
—Book of Proverbs 20:1, *The Holy Bible*

SPANIARDS HAVE A REAL REVERENCE FOR FOOD. A meal is an exercise of community spirit, for everyone gathered to enjoy the food and the company.

Spanish cuisine is as varied as Spanish landscapes and climates and some palates may be offended by the generous use of olive oil and garlic in many Spanish dishes. But be adventurous. Spain has produced a cuisine that is as rich in flavour as it is in history, an inspired combination of the very exotic and the very simple. You will surely find something to suit your taste amongst the local dishes. Of course, these days there are lots of Continental (French, German, Belgian, etc.) and Eastern (Chinese, Indian, Indonesian, etc.) foods that are also available.

Rice, which is now a staple food, was first introduced to Spain by Moorish invaders. They also brought spices such as saffron, cumin and anise, fruit such as figs, oranges, lemons and bananas and nuts such as almonds. The New World provided aubergines, tomatoes, potatoes, red and green peppers (both hot and sweet) and chocolate.

Spaniards eat seasonally, relying on the simple excellence of natural resources. The wide geographic range of the country results in the production of vegetables of all types which, for size, flavour and freshness, are hard to beat. Some food, such as sweetcorn, was originally grown specifically for export because Spaniards thought of corn as cattle fodder. These days it is available in most supermarkets. Fruit

Grapes galore at the weekly open-air market. All the fruit and vegetables in the markets are locally grown, and you can get very good bargains.

varieties include apples and strawberries, custard apples and persimmons, many types of grapes, citrus fruits and melons, just to name a few. All these are grown more 'naturally' than in most other countries. Spaniards insist on their produce being not only the freshest, but also as 'natural' as possible. Large, lumpy half-green tomatoes are chosen for salads rather than the neat uniformly red ones (now also available) because of their superior flavour.

Typical Dishes

- *Gazpacho* is a cold tomato-based soup usually served with finely chopped cucumber, tomato, green pepper and croutons.
- *Paella* rice seasoned with saffron is combined with chicken, vegetables and seafood, or sausages, rabbit and meat with chickpeas. Each region had its own variation.
- *Cocido, potaje* or *escudella* is a Spanish stew, usually containing various combinations of meat, fresh and dried vegetables.
- *Bacalao,* a dried salt fish, is still considered a staple food and a popular substitute for meat during Lent when meat is not eaten.
- *Tapas,* an age-old custom in Spain, consists of small portions of a variety of delicacies. It is available in bars and sampled with drinks before dinner.
- *Huevos flamencos* are fried eggs baked with ham, tomatoes and vegetables. Traditionally a dish from Seville, it is now available all over Spain.
- *Empanadas* are small double crusted pies coloured with saffron and stuffed with an array of fillings. Small ones are called *empanadillos*.
- *Churros,* deep-fried strips of dough, are normally served with a cup of hot chocolate.

CONVENIENCE FOOD

Convenience food is another aspect of Spanish eating habits. Spaniards prefer to eat fresh food, bought and prepared each day rather than canned or convenience food. Their diet, according to a recent medical report, is healthier than that

Fruit and vegetables are an important part of the Spanish diet.

of any other Western nation. If you come from a country where convenience food is the norm, the range available in Spain is likely to disappoint you.

GASTRONOMIC DELIGHTS

Spaniards will drive many miles to find a particular restaurant where a local speciality is being offered. Because some foreigners find it difficult to adapt to Spain's idiosyncratic meal times, especially if they have children with them, it is assumed that they are unadventurous and have no interest in food. However, if you consider yourself a gourmet and are prepared to make some effort, you will not be disappointed. Outstanding food is more likely to be found in a village off the beaten track than in a luxury tourist restaurant. Restaurants which open before traditional times tend to cater to the blander international taste.

EVERYDAY FARE
El desayuno (Breakfast)

Most Spaniards are satisfied with a breakfast consisting of coffee and a croissant, a roll or a small sponge bun. A fun alternative (but fattening!) is *churros*, strips of deep-fried dough sprinkled with sugar and dipped into a cup of thick hot chocolate. A great way to start the day!

La comida del mediodia or el almuerzo (Lunch)

Usually considered the main meal of the day, lunch is eaten between 2:00 pm and 4:00 pm. In city restaurants, you will have three courses starting with vegetables, soup, salad, smoked fish or cured meat. Next will be a plate of meat or fish and finally a dessert (*postre*) which can be a flan or ice cream, but most typically will be a piece of fresh fruit. Foreigners are sometimes surprised that the main course may be accompanied only by potatoes.

The lunch break being a lengthy one, most office workers go to a restaurant and have the *menu del dia* (set meal of the day).

Designated Meal Times

It is, of course, important to remember that meal times in Spain are a good bit later than in most other countries... the midday meal is seldom served before 2:00 pm and the evening meal before 9:00 pm. Breakfasts used to be the 'continental' type, serving only coffee or chocolate with a small roll or bun. Nowadays, however, influenced by the influx of foreigners, hotels will serve fruit juices, fruit and even boiled eggs, and some restaurants are willing to cater to people wanting to eat at earlier hours. However, you may find yourself eating in solitary splendour should you venture into a restaurant before the approved hour, especially in areas where tourists are far less common.

Menu del Dia

By law, most Spanish restaurants are required to offer a *menu del dia* of three courses priced at 80 per cent of what each course would cost separately. This *menu del dia* might be chalked up on a blackboard outside for all to see, or you might have to ask for it. In the latter case, it will probably offer the least appetising choices to encourage you to order something fancier from the à la carte menu.

La comida (Dinner)

Spaniards eat dinner quite late in the evening, at about 9:00 pm. This will consist of another three courses, sometimes with a lighter dish replacing the meat course.

Churros sprinkled with sugar are great with coffee or hot chocolate. They are very popular at open-air markets.

Nowadays most people find two such large meals too much and will replace one with snacks at a tapas bar or a sandwich at a fast food café.

Spanish Coffee

Spaniards drink their coffee very strong. It can be served in a variety of ways:

- *Café solo* is strong coffee in a small cup.
- *Café con leche* is coffee diluted with hot milk in a big cup.
- *Café cortado* is coffee diluted with milk and served in a small glass.
- *Café Americano* is not a special brew from America! It is a *café solo* diluted with water served in a big cup especially to suit the American palate. When ordering one, don't ask for an Americano without prefacing it with a café or you might earn yourself a very strange look from the waiter!

REGIONAL SPECIALITIES

Every region has a speciality of its own but *paella* is one which appears in a variety of forms in most parts of Spain. Consisting mainly of rice seasoned with saffron, it can be a combination of chicken, vegetables and seafood, or a combination of sausages, rabbit and meat with chickpeas. Each region will have its own variation. Spaniards usually eat *paella* at midday and preferably at a restaurant by the beach, but it is served to tourists at dinner time too.

Although many people consider *paella* the most typical of Spanish dishes, its origins are fairly recent. The first *paella* was prepared in Valencia in the late 19th century.

The Spanish dish which many claim to be most national or traditional is a meat stew called *cocido* in Madrid, *potaje* in Andalusia and *escudella* by the Catalans. Three basic ingredients—meats, legumes and vegetables—produce a dish usually served in three courses. The broth is served first, then the vegetables, and the meal ends with the different varieties of meat which Spaniards sometimes shred and mix to form what is called *pringa*.

SEAFOOD

Northern Spain is famous for its seafood. One of its specialities is *merluza* (hake), prepared in two ways: either *a la gallega* (steamed in a Galician paprika sauce) or *a la sidra* (in a tangy Asturian cider sauce).

Scallops, the symbol of pilgrims to Santiago, and *pulpo* (fried octopus) are popular in Galicia which is also famous for its oysters, lobsters and crabs. Trout and salmon are a treat in Asturias (a region also famous for its hearty stews).

Basque cuisine, arguably the best in Spain, combines the use of fresh fish from the Atlantic with delicious sauces, doubtless the result of its proximity to France. *Changurro* (stuffed king crab) is a speciality of this area where you will also find an interesting fish dish called *bacalao al pil-pil* (cod fried in garlic and covered in a green sauce made from the fish gelatin).

Spaniards do enjoy their food, so if you are in doubt about what to order, it is usually safe to go along with the waitress' suggestions. Pleasant surprises await you if you are adventurous and try the recommendations. Local trout

Fish is a favourite ingredient in Spanish cooking. The number of fishermen on the *costas* ensure a steady supply of seafood.

cooked *a la llosa* on a slate slab over hot coals is a delicious speciality in the Pyrenees and Western Andalusia is renowned for shrimps, prawns and crayfish, as well as excellent fried fish (crisp on the outside and extremely succulent within).

MEATS AND HAMS

The classic dishes in Castile are *cordero* (lamb) or *cochinillo* (suckling pig) roasted in wood or clay ovens. Casa Botin in Madrid, called the world's oldest restaurant by the *Guinness Book of Records*, specialises in both and the establishment still cooks in ovens which date back over several centuries.

The mountainous districts of Salamanca are famous for their hams and sausages. The cured hams of Trevelez and Jabugo, the *chorizo* (spicy paprika sausage) and *morcilla* (blood sausage) of Granada and Burgos are also renowned. Game is abundant throughout the northern provinces. Meat cooked *a la llosa* is characteristic in the Pyrenees where *civet*, an aromatic stew prepared with wild boar or goat, can also be found.

The food of Extremadura is true peasant fare conditioned by poverty. Pigs form its basis and no parts are spared, including the *criadillas* (testicles). The *charcuterie* products are excellent, notably the cured hams from Montanchez. Certain dishes may appal foreigners as well as Spaniards from other parts of Spain, particularly those dishes involving *ranas* (frogs) and *lagartos* (lizards), the latter usually served with an almond sauce.

CHEESES
Usually only to be bought in the areas where they are made, the range of Spanish cheeses is impressive. However, this range cannot be compared with the variety available in either France or England. Most of the cheeses are grouped together and simply called *Manchego*. A good *Manchego viejo* is almost the equal of Italian Parmesan. In addition to the *Manchegos*, the hard cheeses of La Mancha are delightful when well matured, and *Cabrales*—a cheese made from sheep rather like Roquefort—is worth looking out for.

SWEETS
It may surprise you to discover that convents supply a variety of almond- or honey-based sweets, pastries and cakes. St

Teresa devised *yemas* (egg-yolk sweets) which were originally distributed to the poor. However, their production became a profitable industry for the nuns, so now you can ring the bell of the convent, greet the nun (usually hidden) with *"Ave Maria Purissima"* and, after this formality, proceed to order your *yemas* or *bizcochos* (sponge biscuits) or whatever else may appear on the list pinned to the entrance of the convent. They are usually all delicious.

EATING OUT

Having a meal out is one of the most popular forms of socialising. To Spaniards, eating is not merely a matter of physical necessity but a real source of pleasure. Don't be surprised to see whole families gathered round a table with small children sitting in their mother's lap and elderly grandparents joining in the fun. Mentally or physically handicapped members of the clan are often included in such social outings.

Restaurants

In most Spanish restaurants, standards will vary, as will the prices of food and wine, from exclusive, expensive, immaculately served meals in beautiful surroundings to small, more intimate, usually family-run affairs where the service can be extremely slow during high season. A single waiter (usually the son) races from table to table whilst Papa takes the orders and Mama (assisted by the daughter) deals with the kitchen. They are doing their best, so getting impatient with delays is a waste of time.

In most instances, it is advisable to book a table for whatever time you want to eat. You may have to wait a while, but at least you will be certain of getting a table. Most restaurants nowadays are prepared to start serving meals quite early. However, if you do not want to be surrounded by other foreigners and prefer a more Spanish ambience, remember that locals seldom have lunch before 2:00 pm or even 3:00 pm and dinner before 9:00 pm or 10:00 pm.

In the family-run bar or restaurant, don't be shocked if your food is brought to the table by the eight-year-old son or daughter of the owner. As young children cannot be left at home unsupervised, they often spend their evenings with Mama and Papa in the restaurant. Rather than allowing the children to get bored with nothing to do, the parents may encourage them to participate in the running of the family business.

Merenderos

'Cheap and cheerful' best describes these numerous small country restaurants which usually serve meals outdoors in the summer. Some may have a set menu giving you a choice of appetiser, main course and dessert, with half a bottle of wine or mineral water going for as little as 6 euros per person (about £ 4 or US$ 7). The house wines are drinkable, but you may prefer to pay a bit more and order one you like better.

Tapas Bars

Perhaps most typical of Spain, these bars are favourite meeting places for young and old alike. Some display the day's offerings in dishes ranged along the top of the counter, others will merely have a blackboard up on a wall listing the goodies on offer. You either sit at the bar and make your selection there, or find yourself a table and what you order will be brought to you.

The selection can be a gastronomic delight: thinly sliced aubergines or courgettes dipped in light batter and deep fried; whole mushrooms or thinly sliced artichokes grilled with lemon, oil and garlic; grilled sardines, crisply fried *pescaditos* or *boccarones* (small fish of different types); *almeja* (mussels and tiny clams) or *calamares* (squid) either *a la plancha* (grilled whole) or *a la romana* (cut into rings and deep fried in batter); crispy salads; delicious meatballs or a simple *tortilla* which is an omelette made with potatoes and garlic. It's a good idea to ask the waiter if there are any 'specials' available. One evening we feasted on sardines, deboned, opened flat, dipped in light batter and deep fried.

Tapas Delights

Most visitors find *tapas* bars a treat as they are given an opportunity to try any number of different typical dishes. But nowadays, including wine, the bill seldom comes to less than 10 euros per person.

BAR IMPERIAL

Beba
Coca-Cola

Tapas bars tucked away in back streets may look ordinary but are worth checking out. Here, you can have an enjoyable meal, and sample various Spanish dishes in small portions.

Tipping

If you are satisfied with the service in a restaurant, a 10 per cent tip is adequate. If you eat *tapas* at a bar, the tip is usually less and it is usual to round off the bill to the nearest euro. Incidentally, whilst on the subject of tipping, taxi drivers and hotel porters will expect small tips for carrying your luggage. Barbers usually expect one euro for a haircut and ladies' hairdressers twice that amount for a wash and set.

Eating Out

The last time we stopped at a hotel in San Sebastian, we came down to the dining room at 9:30 pm to find it completely empty apart from the waitresses. When we asked to see the menu, the waitress serving us shrugged her shoulders and reeled off the evening's offerings. However, her 'Spanish' (*Euskera*, the Basque language) was such that we didn't understand one word. We shrugged in turn and nodded our acceptance, and a plate of spinach cooked with garlic appeared in front of us. It didn't look too wonderful but tasted delicious. Next came a clay pot filled with fish cooked with tomatoes, onions and aubergines, and finally a small bowl full of luscious black cherries. By the time we were drinking our coffee, the restaurant was packed with Spaniards, all eating exactly what we had had with evident gusto.

Restaurant Etiquette

When eating out, you may see the ladies of the restaurant party grouped together at one end of the table and all the menfolk at the other. This is because, until recently, Spanish women rarely mixed socially with Spanish men.

DRINKING

Although Spaniards are comparatively heavy drinkers—they may start the day off with a *carajillo* (black coffee laced with a large tot of brandy) for breakfast, polish off a bottle of wine with their *bocadillo* (sandwich) at lunch time and sit in the bars drinking all evening—you will seldom see a drunken Spaniard.

Prices of local wines, liqueurs and brandies are extremely cheap and this sometimes gives foreigners a headache… literally! Particular care should be taken when ordering a whisky, gin or rum-based drink… the price may seem

Paella, a wonderful dish of rice cooked with seafood, chicken and aromatic herbs and spices, is considered by many foreigners to be the Spanish 'National Dish'.

comparatively high but the measure you get will be far more generous than you may be used to!

A pleasant summer drink is *sangria*, a fruit and wine punch diluted with lemonade but sometimes given a 'kick' by the addition of one or two stronger alcohols. Don't order *sangria* if you are in a 'low dive' because it may be laced with very cheap, poor-quality alcohol which is quite likely to make you ill.

Catalonia is the home of the exceptional Catalan *cava*, a sparkling wine still made in the traditional manner, with a taste and quality which is able to compete with French champagne.

On the whole, Spaniards are unpretentious in their drinking habits, buying their wines from huge barrels marked *tinto* (red), *blanco* (white) or *rosado* (pink). However, recent promotion of Spanish wines has made them fashionable, and bottles are now labelled in accordance with other European standards, stating the year of the production rather than the 'age' in so many years.

Spain's largest wine-growing area, La Mancha, produces the cheaper variety of wine from Valdepenas. At the other end of the scale are the excellent red wines from Rioja, some of which have a full-bodied, woody flavour from being matured for up to eight years in casks made of oak.

Sherries have, of course, always been popular with Spaniards and foreigners alike. However, the English have dominated the sherry trade in Jerez de la Frontera since the 16th century. Many of the labels are foreign—Harvey and Sandeman, for example. Classic dry sherry is called *fino*; *amontillado* is deeper in colour and taste; and *oloroso* is more like a sweet dessert wine. Another aperitif is *manzanilla*, a fortified wine with a faint tang of the sea. Sherries are considered an ideal accompaniment to *tapas* but many Spaniards will also drink them with their meals.

Spanish brandies make a perfect ending to a Spanish meal but you may prefer to try an *anis* (a drink which tastes of aniseed), either *seco* (dry) or *dulce* (sweet). A popular after-dinner drink is called *sol y sombra* (sun and shade). It

Alcohol is generally cheaper in Spain than elsewhere in Europe. Spanish wines are very high quality and can be purchased from local corner shops.

is a combination of brandy and *anis* and the proportions can be varied to suit your taste. Another popular drink is a sweet liqueur called *ponche caballero* which comes in a silver-coated bottle.

TABLE MANNERS

Spaniards, like most continentals, eat with the fork in the left hand and the knife in the right. Food is cut and pushed on the fork with the knife and the fork is then lifted, upside down, to the mouth. Neither fingers nor bread are used to put food onto a fork or into the mouth. Wrists are kept on the table and it is considered bad manners not to have both hands visible at all times. At a dinner party, the guest of honour is seated to the right of the host with the hostess at the other end of the table facing the host. Spaniards hate to see good food wasted and consider it more polite to refuse extra helpings rather than leave food untouched on the plate.

COMMON COURTESY

Enormous areas of Spain are covered in vineyards. The sight of huge bunches of luscious ripe grapes at the end of summer are an enormous temptation to stop the car, hop out and sample a few. The farmer is unlikely to begrudge you a few grapes to sample on the spot but filling up a box or basket to take home with you is another matter. Don't do it unless you are prepared to face an irate farmer! Offering to pay for the grapes might just pacify him.

CULTURE
AND TRAVEL

CHAPTER 7

'When thou art at Rome, do as they do at Rome.'
—Miguel de Cervantes

SPANIARDS WORK HARD, and they also set about their *fiestas* with unlimited enthusiasm. *Fiestas* in Spain are frequent, fun and famous for their fireworks. Spaniards are a happy people and any reason is reason enough for a *fiesta*. Chances are one is being celebrated somewhere in Spain every day of the year.

FIESTAS

'A feast or festivity, holy day or holiday' is the dictionary definition of *fiesta*. This hardly conveys the variety of *fiestas* enjoyed by Spaniards. From the smallest family party gathering to celebrate a birthday, anniversary or First Communion to nationwide holidays such as the Feast Day of St Joseph, *fiestas* are a time for families and friends, a time for all to enjoy themselves, from tiny children to aged grandparents. Relatives and friends will return from all parts of Europe to join the celebration. Men, women and children put on their finest suits and prettiest dresses and go out to have some fun!

Time Off for Fiestas

In addition to this, other breaks in routine are becoming more common. *Puentes* (bridges) develop if a National Holiday happens to fall midweek. This means workers are given time off between the actual *fiesta* and the nearest Sunday, so if a *fiesta* falls on a Tuesday, offices could be shut from the Friday of the preceding week right up until the following Wednesday.

Foreigners sometimes find it frustrating that the holiday periods of Easter, summer and Christmas are times when least work is done in Spain. It is a good idea to get hold of a local diary and take note of all the *fiesta* dates in your area, thus ensuring that you won't run out of cash nor attempt the impossible when transacting business.

Participation

Fiestas are for the people of the whole town or village. Almost everyone takes part. Some posts have been held by members of the same family for generations. The money for the celebrations comes from door-to-door collections or from various other sources—a surplus in the refuse collection account, for example!

When Spaniards celebrate a *fiesta*, they really celebrate. However, foreigners should remember that most *fiestas* have a religious origin and, despite the festive air, the

A Fiesta Menu

Fiestas normally include:
- feasting when lavish meals are served with lots of wine and laughter.
- various kinds of processions depending on the occasion: small children parading in regional costumes; young adults fancily dressed and equipped as Moors and Christians; large and spectacular floats carrying elaborate papier-mâché figures or holy relics.
- music supplied by a single guitar with everyone singing, or village bands parading with the processions, or castanets clattering as background to *flamenco* singing and dancing.
- bullfights, bull running or bull baiting.
- *fallas* (papier-mâché effigies) and a variety of different types of fireworks.

Street dancing is a feature of *fiestas*. These two girls in traditional costume are taking part in the San Juan procession.

occasion is also of religious importance. So don't behave as if it is a funfair.

By nature, Spaniards are loud. They talk loudly, laugh loudly, sing loudly, so of course they will be very noisy during a *fiesta*. Even those participating in the parades and processions are likely to shout greetings to their friends and family along the way. The foreign visitor, however, should not do the same. Unless you are specifically invited to join in, remember you are only a spectator. Be sure not to get in the way of any parade or procession. Spaniards love children and sweets are often given out; but if presents are being distributed, do not expect one as your due. The Three Kings throw handfuls of sweets to the crowds lining the roadside during their procession but do not grab at them greedily, even if they land at your feet. It is better to pick them up and hand them to the nearest children. Although Spaniards are friendly and welcoming by nature, they may not like having you intrude in what they may consider to be specifically their event, so be discreet.

Gigantes And Cabezudos

In certain towns, *gigantes* (giants) and *cabezudos* (big heads) are worn and paraded during *fiestas*. These 'giants' and 'big heads' are grotesque figures, some up to 4.88 m (16 ft)

Papier-mâché figures, depicting well-known personalities or folk heroes, are paraded in the streets before being set alight on the final night of the San Juan fiesta.

in height, some only a little taller than a man. Most of the figures are terrifying; some are very old, having been kept by the townspeople for generations. In Pamplona, these huge images representing Moors and Normans visit the town hall, dance before the cathedral and pay their respects to their patron saint, San Fermín, on 7 July when bulls are let loose in the streets. The public joins in and casualties are sometimes fatal.

Fallas

Some *fiestas* date back to very early days and have a pagan element about them. Coinciding with the summer solstice, the fire celebrations, which take place nationally on the night of San Juan, are a reminder of pre-Christian rites. The *fallas* of Valencia are of this type. Huge papier-mâché sculptures, usually representing politicians and public figures, displayed in the streets for a week. Some can be quite obscene and even phallic. All are set alight at midnight to enormous bonfires and the fireworks which follow spectacular and sometimes frightening to those used to such entertainment!

Bull Running

If you are not accustomed to village *fiestas*, beware! Your introduction could be a bull chasing you down a narrow street. Barricades are erected in order to keep the bulls confined. However, unwary strangers have been known to duck under or climb over them only to find themselves suddenly faced with charging bulls. To avoid what must seem almost certain mutilation—if not death—they may, in desperation, climb the nearest lamppost or dive through an open window, possibly landing in the lap of a beaming old Spaniard, watching such antics with amusement from the safety of his house.

Macho Men

Spaniards consider bull running a national sport; the young and not so young men of the village will tease and encourage bulls to chase them down the narrow streets to enhance their 'macho' image. Occasionally such bravado backfires and someone gets hurt, but quite often the only bulls available are bored and docile beasts used year after year and therefore quite disciplined to 'perform' as so desired.

Pamplona

The bulls which run in Pamplona during the July *fiesta* of San Fermin should not be teased by the unwary. These bulls are bred for courage, stamina and ferocity, primarily for the

bullring. Only the young and very fit should risk running with them. Casualties occur each year and some have even proved fatal.

Bull Baiting

Some ports have their bull running on docks which are barricaded at one end with seawalls and thus provide suitable seating for spectators. This is really bull baiting as the beasts need to be encouraged. Firecrackers and tin cans are flung at the feet of the bored animal to make it charge after the youngster who jumps out of the way. With luck, the animal's momentum will carry it over the edge of the dock into the sea, much to the amusement of the spectators. You might not approve but the bulls appear to enjoy their swim and are carefully craned up out of the water onto the dock side.

Spaniards taking part in such a pastime most certainly do not consider it in the least cruel, so you would be wise to keep your own counsel if you do not like the spectacle.

Nowadays, foreigners of both sexes are encouraged to join in the fun but pre-teenagers attempting to enter the enclosure are politely, but firmly, discouraged... after all, this could be a dangerous game and accidents have been known to happen.

Bullfighting

Many foreigners consider this sport cruel and unfair to the bulls, in fact, decidedly shocking. To Spaniards, it is an art form comparable to ballet, combining courage and technique on the part of the bullfighter, and stamina and cunning on the part of the bull. Not recommended for sensitive souls with queasy stomachs, the pageantry and spectacle of the serious bullfights can be breathtakingly beautiful. *Aficionados* (fans) watching are enthralled, but despite being aroused and excited, never resort to acts of violence.

Occasionally, the tables are turned. One bull was seen going into a ring with such energy that it jumped over the barricades into the tiers of seating. The *aficionados* sitting there had no option but to leap into the ring, leaving the bewildered bull to race around the seats! This, however, is very unusual and could only happen in one of the smaller, more provincial rings.

Moors and Christians (Morros Y Cristianos)

Many villages commemorate the battles between the Christians and Arabs during the Reconquest of Spain. Mock battles are staged over a three-day period with one army wearing chain-mail made of fabric to avoid being overcome by heat exhaustion. Otherwise their opponents dressed in togas would win too easily. The Christians take possession of the 'castle' and the Moors counter-attack the next day when the whole village becomes a battleground. On the final day, the Banner of the Cross is victorious.

Participants are often seen in the village bars fortifying themselves for the next stage of the battle. A foreigner might be alarmed to see one army bodily throwing their enemies out of a bar amidst blood-curdling yells, but Spaniards love this type of *fiesta*. Whole families will turn out to watch the processions (the costumes are elaborate and often breath-takingly beautiful) and bands, take part in the dancing in the streets, and to see unsuspecting foreigners leap into the air when firecrackers explode at their feet.

Ferias

'A fair or market', *feria* usually refers to a gathering for the sale and purchase of bulls and/or horses. The Spanish talent for enjoyment turns many *ferias* into *fiestas* and they draw similar crowds; parades and processions, singing and dancing create the same excitement.

Although many cities are famous for the beauty and splendour of their celebrations, the *feria* in Seville at Easter is perhaps the most memorable of all with its gathering of *gitanos* dressed in their traditional long flounced, brilliant spotted dresses and Spanish nobility parading their fine horses.

Romerias (Pilgrimage Excursion)

The most popular *romeria* (pilgrimage excursion) in Spain takes place in Andalusia in honour of the Virgin of El Rocio. People come from all over Spain, on horseback and in flower-covered wagons and carriages, to make their way to the shrine of the Virgin of El Rocio in Almonte. Many days are devoted to prayer, offerings, celebrating mass along with song and dance and wine-drinking. At dawn on the final day, the statue of the Virgin of El Rocio is removed from its shrine and solemnly paraded through the crowded streets.

A Word Of Warning

The *feria* is a fairground in every sense of the word and foreigners should be warned about pickpockets and con men. To avoid a possibly unpleasant experience, leave your jewellery locked up at home and make sure your handbag is securely held. You should take the same precautions even when merely walking around the weekly village open-air markets. A few years ago, mugging and bag-snatching were unusual but, nowadays, one hears of daring snatches in broad daylight, particularly in areas where gypsies abound. Even when you think you are securely protected in your car with the windows shut, do not be complacent. Windows have been smashed and bags snatched from the laps of surprised passengers. On one occasion, a car was being driven slowly through Valencia, traffic being particularly heavy because it was a *fiesta*, when the back door was opened and a youth reached in and grabbed the handbag which was firmly jammed between the front seats. By the time the driver and his passenger had freed themselves from their seat belts, the youth was nowhere in sight.

It would be unjust to imply that gypsies are responsible for all burglaries. On the *costas* north of Andalusia, foreign summer visitors have been known to enter houses where windows are invitingly left open to snatch what cash may be lying about.

Christmas

Until recently, Christmas was not celebrated with as much enthusiasm in Spain as in most other countries. The death and resurrection of Christ at Easter was considered far more important in Spanish observances than his birth. It used to be impossible to buy Christmas cards in Spain, and turkeys were unheard of, Spaniards preferring a leg of lamb. Father Christmas or St Nicolas, who traditionally brings toys for the children on Christams Day, made his first appearance in Spain on a Kodak billboard in the late 1970s. As with everything else, times have changed and Christmas trees, cards and presents are now easily available in most areas.

New Year's Eve

You may find yourself wondering what to do with the 12 grapes handed to you just before midnight on New Year's Eve. Spanish custom expects you to swallow one grape each time the clock strikes the midnight hour. If you manage to down them all at the correct moment, you have earned yourself good luck for the coming year. If no grapes are available, you may be given a handful of raisins for the same purpose. But be careful! Small, dry raisins are even more difficult to swallow in quick succession than juicy grapes.

Los Reyes Magos (Twelfth Night)

In some parts of Spain, 6th January is celebrated as Los Reyes Magos (Twelfth Night), the time when the procession of The Three Kings takes place. It is the grand finale to all the Christmas and New Year festivities. The three young men chosen to portray The Three Kings consider it such an honour that they will happily go into debt to make the occasion a memorable one. One young man sold his flat in order to have sufficient funds to pay for the costumes and the entertainment which are an essential part of being selected as one of the Kings.

Children are given their main presents on Twelfth Night rather than Christmas, and the Kings throw handfuls of sweets as they parade along the streets. The processions and parades of colourful floats and beautifully costumed attendants on this occasion are an impressive sight.

Gifts Galore

On the eve of The Thre children put their shoe porch or balcony in a of gifts. The next m shoes will conta supposedly deli Three Kings duri

Semana Santa (Easter)

Christ's crucifixion and resurrection at Easter is treated with more pomp and ceremony than his birth on Christmas Day. Easter is a time for celebration because it marks the victory of good over evil.

The *Semana Santa* ceremonies which take place during Easter are perhaps the most beautiful and moving of all spectacles, and religious fervour runs high. Foreigners who come to witness these occasions should treat them with great respect. Although the processions and celebrations are spectacular, you should remember their religious content.

Magnificent celebrations are held during Holy Week throughout Spain, especially in Andalusia and in the monasteries of Guadalupe, Escorial and Montserrat. Toledo, Valladolid and Saragossa also celebrate Holy Week with splendour. These celebrations take the form of processions where 'penitents' wearing the distinctively coloured hooded robes of their particular *cofradias* (confraternity or brotherhood) will accompany a pair of sculptured groups, one depicting a scene from the Passion and the other a Mater Dolorosa decked out in jewelled and heavily embroidered vestments. Each of these *pasos* (mobile tableaux), some of which date to the 17th century, is carried on the shoulders of about 100 men chosen for their strength. In Seville, the *pasos* sail through the streets amid clouds of flowers and glittering candles. They are greeted by strident wavering cries of "*Saetas*", impromptu arrows of song of *gitano* or *flamenco* inspiration uttered by gypsies as certain statues pass in front of them. Each will pass through the great cathedral to be blessed before being returned to its chapel.

ENTERTAINMENT

In addition to *fiestas* and *ferias*, you can find the usual type entertainment in the towns and villages of Spain.

ma

a few of the larger cities in Spain have theatres which show foreign films in the original language. You will find these listed in the local papers and marked 'V.O.' for Original Version.

Alternatively, once you have mastered enough Spanish to understand a conversation, you could try one of the local shows. Spanish films are usually of good quality (Spain has produced several world renowned directors and actors) and watching a Spanish film will help you polish up your language skills as well as give you an insight into different aspects of Spanish society.

Late Hours

It can be a surprise to discover that most entertainments do not start until late at night and that you are not likely to get to bed much before dawn. This applies throughout Spain and at all times of the year, not only during *fiestas*. Stamina is required if you want to keep up with the celebrations. It is a curious fact that Spaniards can dance all night and work normally the following day. Perhaps the *siesta* is a habit which foreigners should quickly adopt if they intend to keep Spanish hours.

The Arts

Madrid puts on major arts festivals during all four seasons. Events include world-class jazz, salsa, African music and rock. Film festivals and art exhibitions can be enjoyed at reasonable prices. The venues are quite often city parks or open-air amphitheatres.

English language performances are a rarity but you won't need to know Spanish to enjoy the traditional operettas called *zarzuelas*, a sort of bawdy comedy. Concerts of classical music are very popular and the Auditorio Nacional de Musica in Madrid regularly hosts major orchestras from around the world.

Catalans are great art lovers and Sunday morning concerts in the Palau de la Musica in Barcelona are a popular tradition. The Gran Teatro del Licou is a very fine opera house, considered second only to Milan's La Scala. The season runs from November to March but may occasionally be extended into spring. Compared to New York and London, the prices of tickets are very reasonable.

Flamenco

Without any doubt, Seville and Jerez are the of *flamenco*. The former has three *flamenco*

Come on! Anyone can do a *flamenco*! You will find the most authentic *flamenco* dancers in Andalusia, especially in Seville.

these are patronised mostly by tourists rather than by locals. Although Catalans are not too fond of this purely Andalusian spectacle, there are one or two night spots in Barcelona catering to tour groups, but these can be very expensive.

Flamenco, essentially the creation of Andalusian gypsies, has been shamelessly exploited by the tourist industry. Your best chance of seeing and hearing good *flamenco* is to go to one of the *flamenco* festivals which are held throughout Andalusia during the summer months. These festivals attract the finest performers but they never really get going until the early hours of the morning and quite often last until dawn.

The *flamenco* has many singing styles but the two main nes are *cante chico* (meaning small song) and *cante jondo* eaning deep song). The former is light weight and cheerful the latter passionate and sad.

nas

of music and dancing, stemming from the *Canto* mmonly confused with *flamenco* by foreigners. s a mixture of folk and pop, and is traditionally performed during *ferias*, the spring parties known as Cruzes de Mayo, and the annual pilgrimage to the Virgin of the Rocio. On these occasions of endless singing, dancing and drinking, pleasure is pursued to a degree seldom matched anywhere else in Western society.

Football

Surprisingly enough, football in Spain has more *aficionados* than even bullfighting. It is, in fact, considered to be THE national sport and football supposedly has a greater following in Spain than it does even in England, where the game originated.

The most popular teams are Real Madrid whose home is the 130,000 spectator Santiago Bernabeu Stadium and Atletico Madrid whose Vicente Calderon Stadium is located on the outskirts of town. The best team in the Basque area is the Club Atletico Bilbao and fixtures for games are listed in the local press. Catalans, however, are perhaps the most active of all Spanish *futbol* supporters. When the team from Barcelona, Barça, wins, everyone goes wild with joy. Victory for the team is sometimes celebrated for an hour or more with car horns being tooted, rockets going off and fans waving flags and cheering.

Football matches are played on Saturday and Sunday evenings (to avoid the mid-afternoon heat) and tickets are not considered expensive, at 20 euros for an average seat. The season lasts from September until June and the last match of the season is the Copa Real or 'King's Cup'. All the bars with a television will have a *futbol* match on their screens during the weekend and supporters, unable to acquire tickets for the game, will crowd into bars and scream their pleasure whenever a goal is scored by their team. People gamble on football results through a tote called *Quiniela*.

Futbol sala is the latest craze in nearly all the bigger towns and cities. Run as a commercial business, it is a form of football played indoors, usually in large underground car parks converted for the purpose. A very fast game and highly competitive, teams of youths form for the season and league games are organised.

Even very small villages will have at least one football field which children can use if the local school does not have one. In one small seaside resort on the Costa Blanca, a sum of 60,101.21 euros was approved by the town council for the creation of a football school whereas only one-tenth of that amount was approved to fund a home help service via the Red Cross for the elderly, handicapped or disabled. Teaching children to play football, therefore, would appear to be high on their list of priorities!

TRAVELLING AROUND THE COUNTRY

You can get around Spain in a number of ways, including trains, buses and even bicycles, should you so desire, and there are numerous places of cultural interest throughout the country for you to visit.

In addition to travelling around Spain, visits to some of the neighbouring countries can also be very enjoyable. Portugal on the west and France and Andorra to the north offer opportunities for weekend trips and the chance to sample a change of diet, perhaps, or to go skiing or mountain walking. Morocco and Gibraltar to the south also have their attractions but, in my experience, most people who have a few days' holiday prefer to explore different areas in Spain itself since the country offers a wide choice of camping/biking facilities, horseback treks and suchlike, as well as an interesting variety of different cuisines.

City Safety

Women should be aware of the fact that muggings occur frequently in some areas. Usually it is the elderly and frail who are targeted, often by lads on motor scooters, who drive up close and grab a handbag before accelerating off again. Women coming out of banks are particularly vulnerable. Hitch-hiking is not advisable even if you are not alone. Girls have ɔeen known to accept a ride ɔly to be abducted and taken to ᴣerted mountain areas where ⸃ are eventually murdered. if you think you are used ᷧnking and can handle ⸃, you should be careful. measures tend to be ᷧerous and one alcoholic ⸃ely to be double the ᷧgin, whiskey or rum ᷧsed to.

LEISURE OCCUPATIONS (HOBBIES)

Because a large part of the population, particularly in the coastal areas and larger towns, consists of retired people, more time and money are spent in the field of sport rather than on other forms of amusement.

Water Sports

Sailing and boating are very popular along the Mediterranean coast and there are hundreds of marinas and clubs available. Spain's best-known sailing enthusiast is King Juan Carlos who keeps his fleet of boats in Majorca.

Most resort beaches will have areas designated for wind surfing or water- and jet-skiing. This makes the swimming safer for those who are not interested in such sports. Scuba-diving and underwater fishing are very popular, but make sure your presence in the water is clearly indicated with a marker buoy.

Winter Sports

Excellent skiing and winter sports facilities are s·
throughout Spain's mountainous regions, from th·
Europa in the west across to the Pyrenees which c·
resorts such as Baqueira-Beret near Lerida a·
in Aragon. You can also ski close to Madrid ·
Valcoto and Valdesqui, and at Solynieve in r·

probably the most popular area. Costs for skiing in Spain are much lower than at any of the continental resorts, and accommodation and food are also more reasonably priced.

Mountaineering and climbing are also popular and there are plenty of challenges throughout Spain in terms of difficulty of ascent. However, don't expect the rescue backup service that you would get in the rest of Europe. In Spain, climbing is an individual affair and carried out at your own risk. Better join a club and check out local conditions before setting off. Remember that brown bears and wolves still exist and they may not enjoy being disturbed, so take care!

Hunting

Spain is famous as a 'paradise' for hunters due to its climatic range, the variety of its wildlife and the many traditional methods of hunting both large and small game. Numerous national parks and game preserves exist where natural resources are protected. Big game includes deer, stag, ibex, roebuck, mountain goat, boar, wolf, mountain sheep, bear and lynx. The latter is completely protected having become scarce, and hunting bears is restricted.

There are literally thousands of private reserves for small game where most of the hunting takes place. Among the small game you will find partridge, water fowl, dove, quail, bustard, grouse, rabbit, hare and pheasant.

Many traditional methods of hunting exist in Spain—some on horseback, some on foot, others involving groups of hunters with horses, assistants, hounds and handlers. However, the only method permitted in the national reserves and game preserves is called *resecho* where a single hunter, sometimes accompanied by a guide, searches for game on foot, a true test of his knowledge and physical ability.

Small game is sought by a lone hunter who will shoot at anything his dog starts. The most popular method used in hunting the Spanish red partridge is 'beating up'. Preparing for such an occasion requires great knowledge of the partridge and the terrain which is divided into plots, in each of which a dozen or so blinds are set up. In these partridge drives, nothing is left to chance. Everything is calculated and arranged so that helpers, loaders, beaters and hunters all come together at the right time and in the right place. This type of Spanish hunt is internationally famous and, unless you have taken part in one of these traditional drives, you really shouldn't boast about being a 'hunter' in Spain!

Shooting

Many foreigners are shocked by the sight of hundreds of small dead birds piled on the side of country roads and wonder if such slaughter is really necessary. The excuse for this seemingly indiscriminate massacre is that farmers a protecting crops on their fruit trees. However, the sight c many little corpses lying by the roadside leaves one wi impression that local 'huntsmen' are amusing thems blasting away at anything that flies. If you are fond in the hills, you should make sure you don't areas where such 'huntsmen' abound.

Black and white signs hanging from trees or in forests saying *Coto privado de caz* hunting area'. So it is advisable to keep

You can fish from almost any part of the Spanish shoreline.

Fishing

With its 4,964 km (3,084.49 miles) of coastline and more
than 20 times as many miles of rivers and streams, plus
all the dams and reservoirs scattered around the country,
Spain offers unlimited possibilities for the keen fisherman.
Spanish salmon rivers are found throughout the Cantabrian
range and along the coast of Galicia, and trout can be caught
in the upper reaches of practically any river in Spain. Salt-
water fishing can be done from the shore, or from boats,
or underwater. All forms of fishing require licences and can
only be pursued during open seasons, with limitations on
minimum sizes.

ening

rs are available as 'professional' Spaniards or
foreigners, but many people prefer to do their own
his can be an extremely rewarding pastime. But
of warning—do not try and grow all kinds of
usually found in your area unless you are
pointments. It's safer to have a garden full
flowers which can cope with the local

weather conditions without too much attention, and indulge your desire for exotics by keeping them in pots.

On occasion, you may find caterpillar nests high up in the branches of one of your trees. These look like large footballs of dirty cotton wool and are unsightly in themselves. They are home to caterpillars with strange habits. When the caterpillars leave the nest, they will travel in long lines, nose to tail. If disturbed, they produce an irritant which can cause redness and swelling and which is extremely harmful around the eyes and mouth. The only way to rid yourself of the nests is by tying some cloth soaked in petrol to a long pole and then setting it and the nest on fire. This is a dangerous exercise, since pine trees are highly inflammable.

Pine Trees

If you are a keen gardener, there are one or two things about pine trees you should know. Pine trees can generate passionate support from some people, and equally passionate hatred from others. When the original vineyards covering certain parts of the coastal areas eventually died from old age, the terraces they occupied were in many cases planted with pine trees, purely as a measure of soil conservation. The resulting pine forests now cover enormous areas.

When we bought our *parcela* (plot) some thirty years ago, the first thing that had to be done was to get rid of enough pines (which at that time were no more than 10 ft or 3 m high) to make room for the house. Romantic notions about pines dictated that a minimum number of trees were cut down and this proved to be a big mistake. We soon discovered that pine trees covering hillsides may look lovely and green and conserve the soil, but pine trees growing in one's garden are a different matter.

They not only drink all available water which makes grow at a fantastic speed, but they shed thousands of with great regularity, covering the ground so nothing ever grows beneath their branches. Th matter of pine pollen. The first time we fou and verandas covered in a thick yellow dismayed but not disheartened. However that sweeping up this yellow menace was a waste of time as more would settle in the next few days. This lasts several weeks early in the year. For people suffering from allergies, pine pollen can become quite a problem.

FOREST FIRES

In the past, most forest fires were accidental. In recent years there have been more deliberately set fires. Should there be a wind, the trees catch fire and explode into flame. Controlling such conflagrations becomes extremely hazardous. Recently, Spanish forests have suffered several damaging fires. Never drop a cigarette butt out of your car window, and never leave a garden fire unattended.

COMMUNICATING

CHAPTER 8

'What's in a name? That which we c
any other name would smell
—William Shakesp

BASED ON LATIN SPREAD BY THE ROMANS, Spanish is a Romance language. What the world accepts as Spanish is in fact *Castellano* (Castilian), originally the dialect of the kingdom of Castile. It is the official language in Spain used by the majority of the mass media and also in official documents.

PECULIARITIES
Castilian Lisp
In central Spain and a few points north, a distinctive lisp is pronounced with the letters 's', soft 'c' when followed by 'e' or 'i', and 'z'. *Gracias* (Thank you) becomes *GRAH-thee-ahs* and Aragon's capital *Saragossa* becomes *THAH-rah-gotha*. Everywhere else in Spain, the soft 'c' and 'z' are pronounced normally, but it is interesting to note that, as Castilian is thought of as a 'high Spanish', the most prestigious form, the lisp is ften used in areas where it normally would not apply.

everal theories exist as to how and why the Castilian volved, the most popular explanation being that a certain Castilian king spoke with a lisp. His courtiers, wanting to be like the king, imitated him, and it became a popular way of talking.

alects

al dialects
wed and
0s that
more
ach
ir
f

An organisation called the Real Academia de la Lengua Espanola acts as the governing body of the Spanish language. It determines the accepted spelling of words, ruling whether new words can be considered proper Spanish or not. It also produces the *Diccionario de la lengua española de la Real Academia Española* (Dictionary of the Spanish Language of the Royal Spanish Academy) that is considered the ultimate linguistic authority in Spain and Latin America.

Pronunciation Guide

There are four basic rules:

- Pronounce every syllable distinctively
- Stress the right syllable
- Keep consonants soft
- Keep vowels short

Vowels:

- a   as in *far*, never as in *tape*
- e   as *they* but never as in *Pete*
- i   always as *ee*
- o   as in *hope* but like *hop* in an enclosed syllable
- u   always as *oo* but silent after *q* as in *que* or *qui*

Semivowels:

- i, y   as the *y* in *yes*
- u   unstressed *u* between consonant and vowel

Diphthongs:

- ai, ay   the same as *i* in *ride*
- au   as *ou* in *shout*
- ei, ey   the same as *ey* in *grey*
- eu   with *e* and *u* pronounced independently
- oi, oy   just as *oy* in *toy*

Consonants:

- h   is always silent
- j   as in *h*
- s   before *b, d, g, l, m* or *r* like *z*

A Melting Pot

While differences in lifestyle and cultural traditions still exist, the process of assimilation of the Spanish population has gone on for such a long time that identifications of Spain's ethnic groups will soon be based on language alone.

About 17 per cent of the population speak Catalan, 7 per cent speak Galician and 2 per cent speak Basque but there are additional dialects spoken throughout the country such as Valenciano and Aragonese and Andalusian.

LEARNING DIFFICULTIES

These regional languages create enormous difficulties for foreigners travelling from one region to another as road signs can be in the local language, making them hard to decipher if one is not familiar with that particular tongue. This medley of languages can be disconcerting to foreigners who have learned Castilian Spanish, more so because each regional language has different pronunciations and spellings. For instance, who would think that Javea and Xabia are one and the same place? Or that Donostia is the Basque name for San Sebastian? However, with frequent interaction, you will soon distinguish the differences between Castilian and the regional language spoken in your area.

Catalan

Closely related to the Provençal language of southern France, Catalan resembles French more closely in both vocabulary and accent than Castilian. It is derived from the rich languages of the Oc linguistic region in France and is especially suited to poetry and song.

Spoken mostly in Catalonia in the north-eastern part of Spain, subtypes exist such as Valencian or *Valenciano* all down the east coast of Spain. Majorca or Mallorca has individual dialects called *Mallorquin*, which also exist in Minorca and Ibiza and a dialect called *Chapurriano* is spoken in Aragon.

Galician

Closely related to Portuguese, Galician or *Gallego* also has its roots in the Romance languages. Spoken in the north-western area of Spain, it is primarily a rural language and not heard much in the larger cities of the region.

Basque

Spoken in the Basque provinces of Vizcaya, Guipuzcoa and Álava, and even in parts of south-western France, Basque stands out in particular for its unique linguistic characteristics. No one has been able to trace its true origins. It resembles no other language in Spain or, for that matter, any other dialect anywhere else in the world except perhaps that of a small area in the Caucasus Mountains of the former Soviet Union.

Arabic Influence

Having been occupied by the Moors for 750 years, is surprising that in Spain at least 4,000 words and A derived phrases have been absorbed into the S languages. Being well advanced in the study of r science and astronomy, the Moors left a legac many of which have travelled through Spanis languages including French and English (su alcohol, chemistry, nadir, zenith, alkaline ar

SPANISH NAMES

Traditional Spanish names reflect the importance of the family. Women retain their maiden name after marriage. For example, when Eva Peña marries Juan Garcia, she becomes *Señora* Eva Peña de (day) Garcia. Their children's last names would be Garcia Pena. In the next generation, the mother's name would be dropped unless it is a famous one. In correspondence, both last names are used (Sr Garcia Peña) but in conversation only the first name is used.

The first name is considered the most important. Garcia Peña would be listed under 'G' rather that 'P'. Middle names do not exist in Spain where a person might have one or many first names but only two last names.

Children who have the same first name as their father or mother will have the suffix *ito* or *ita* meaning 'little one' added to their name. Juan will become Juanito and Eva will become Evita. *(For more information on Spanish names, refer to the paragraph 'Spanish Surnames' in Chapter 4, Socialising.)*

Addressing Someone

There are two forms of address, formal and infomal. The informal *tu* should only be used when you know someone well, otherwise use *usted*.

NON-VERBAL COMMUNICATION

Most Continentals, Spaniards included, probably use more non-verbal communication than either the British or North Americans. Compared with the French, Spaniards on the whole appear more conservative and less prone to excessive facial expressions and hand gestures. They may wave their hands about in descriptive ways, emphasising whatever they are saying, particularly if they think that you, the foreigner, ʒnnot understand their speech. For instance, when they ˙t you to look at something, they are quite likely to say ˙ʳ!" ("Look!") and simultaneously point at their own eye ˥n at the object you are intended to look at or admire. ˧ 'kiss the air' and shrug their shoulders to indicate ˧mportance', and they may wag a finger in the air ˧on't do that!'
ˣously insulting gestures, generally understood ˥ensive in most other countries are used

in Spain but are commonly avoided, except in the most provocative of situations.

Amongst the older generations, Spaniards are still extremely self-contained and dignified. Displays of affection between the sexes in public, for instance, would be considered in very poor taste, apart of course from the kisses exchanged as greetings or farewells.

Handshakes are never prolonged and only used at first introductions, after which kissing becomes the accepte form of greeting and/or farewell.

POLITE SPEECH

Spaniards are more courteous and formal in their than most other nationalities, and the foreigne more help and cooperation if he behaves Although Spaniards are capable of infuria' they can be rude, forget to answer ' totally ignore appointments—face-to-f very agreeable.

You may not always be greeted with more than a hard stare from certain officials but, in most instances, you will be treated to a smile and a greeting which will vary according to the time of day and the formality of the occasion.

Greetings

Encantado (Pleased to meet you) is a useful word to know. On informal occasions, *Buenas dias* (Good morning) and *Buenas tardes* (Good afternoon) while daylight lasts and *Buenas noches* (Good night) after twilight may all be shortened to *Buenas* alone. There are a number of ways of saying goodbye: *Buenos* is sometimes used when departing, but *Adios* is more correct. *Hasta la vista* implies "See you again soon", equivalent to the American "So long".

Spaniards may greet total strangers when they enter a restaurant and wish the other diners "*Que aproveche!*" ("Enjoy your meal!") to which "*Usted gusta?*" ("Won't you join us?") used to be the formal response. Social etiquette demanded a refusal with the words "*Muchismas gracias*" ("Many thanks"), whether sincere or not. Nowadays however, this routine formality is rare, and a simple "*Que aproveche!*" or "*Buen provecho!*" is enough to wish others an enjoyable meal.

Please and Thank You

When dealing with the locals, it is far better to err on the side of excessive politeness than to risk being ignored for lack of an expected *Por favor* (Please) or *Gracias* (Thank you).

Por favor can also be used to attract the attention of shop ʒistants who may happily continue to chat to one another ⌐ you stand at the counter waving the item you want to ⌐se under their noses. Saying "Psst!" or whistling would ⌐preciated. In fact, the shop assistant may continue to 'punish' you for your bad manners.

⌐ION

⌐u to discover that there are not too many ʻur hard-learned Spanish will be put to you go shopping or have to deal with ʻappens particularly in the coastal, more touristy areas, where the predominant local population consists chiefly of shopkeepers, fishermen and farmers. They are friendly and helpful but have little in common with the average foreigner. Should you be working in the coastal regions, you would certainly find Spaniards with whom you could socialise but most of the coastal communities divide roughly into national groups, based on linguistic preference. Should you choose to live in a rural area, you would find it much easier to be drawn into village life and, in such cases, you would have ample opportunity to speak Spanish, and even pick up some local dialect.

Urban Spaniards in larger communities like Madrid or Barcelona are, of course, more likely to have common interests with foreigners and, in these circumstances, conversations and friendships can blossom quite rapidly. However these same Spaniards, when they take their holidays at one of the coastal resorts, hardly ever bother to involve themselves with the foreigners residing there. This is understandable. They come for brief holidays to relax with their own families and friends. Trying to sort out foreign residents from foreign tourists simply does not appeal to them. They will be superficially friendly towards all foreigners but do not expect to be received by them in their own homes with open arms.

MAÑANA

If you want to make your stay in Spain a success, the first thing to get used to is *mañana*. This popular word is used frequently by Spaniards, but foreigners should know tha there are several possible meanings. Literally 'tomorro it can also mean 'later' or even 'much later'. It is safe to assume that it does not mean 'today'. This can k infuriating if you are waiting for the electrician o who has assured you that he will come *mañana*

This attitude is not a sign of dishonesty. Sp decrees that a negative answer to your que you come?" is unacceptable. The electricia to disappoint you. Perhaps he really d squeeze a visit to your house into hi schedule, but experience will show that his non-appearance can be really frustrating. You sit at home waiting and no one appears, so you get fed up and venture out. When you come home, you find a note saying the equivalent of "We came! Where were you?" Getting angry with the fellow in question is a waste of time. He will agree with everything you say, smile and tell you he will come *manana, seguro* (tomorrow, for sure). You simply have to learn to be extremely patient. Besides, giving way to anger and frustration will not endear you to the workman in question.

DOING BUSINESS

CHAPTER 9

'Never stand begging for what you have th
—Miguel de Cervantes

WORK PERMITS

If you are coming from a country outside the European Union and want to work in Spain, a work permit obtainable from the Ministry of Labour should be high on your list of priorities. This is applicable to all types of employment, either as an employee of a Spanish company or foreign company or as a self-employed owner of a restaurant/bar or other business. You should never start any enterprise without the necessary permission or licence, or you could find yourself in a very tight corner.

Self-employment

If you work on a self-employed basis, you are still required to join the Spanish social security service, obtain a licence called a *licencia fiscal* and register for Income Tax and IVA. If you are a professional, in most cases, you will have to become member of the appropriate professional college. You may given some exemptions but a written examination is still required.

that Spain has become a full member of the European foreigner from a member country can work freely hout first acquiring a work permit.

'N AN OFFICE

king in Spain can be divided into two hose who work in a Spanish office with

Spaniards, or those who work in an international office surrounded primarily by people of their own nationality. In the former instance, there might be quite a few cultural 'differences' for the foreigner to cope with whilst in the latter case, working conditions in the office would be very similar to those existing in one's home country. The only 'surprises' in the latter case would probably occur in outside dealings with Spanish companies and Spanish business people.

Holiday Months

August is the main holiday month when some offices may close entirely whilst others continue operating on skeleton staff. This could prove frustrating for international companies which wish to continue operating 'as usual'. However, August is 'holiday time' all over Spain and you would therefore do well to arrange your business commitments around the fact that nothing much can be achieved during this holiday period.

- You won't be able to cash money at a bank on Saturday mornings so make sure you have sufficient funds for weekends unless you are prepared to pay the higher rates at other points of exchange.
- At Christmas, the tempo of work begins to slow down from around 6–8 December and most places of work will close at midday on Christmas Eve.
- Boxing Day is not an official holiday but many professional offices will remain closed and not much can be achieved work-wise, in fact, until after Los Reyes Magos (Twelfth Night).
- Some businesses may close down entirely for three weeks around Christmas and New Year.
- At Easter, offices may close at midday on the Thursday preceding Good Friday and stay closed for the weekend, or sometimes even longer.

Spanish Conditions

Spain's employment laws generally favour th
A standard working week is 40 hours with
siesta slowly being replaced by a shorter lun
one-sixth of Spain's 18.82 million worke

unions. Wage levels have been low with the result that many Spaniards used to have more than one job. However, this is now less in evidence as salaries are fast catching up with the rest of Europe.

Employers have to pay high rates for social insurance but do not have to provide pension schemes.

All employees are entitled to 30 days' paid holiday a year in addition to the 15 national public holidays and usually one local public holiday. There are '14 months' in a Spanish employment year because employees are entitled to double salary for the months of June and December. An employee can only be dismissed for old age if it can be proved that his age restricts him from carrying out his job satisfactorily. There is no compulsory retirement age in Spain.

Meetings and Business Lunches

Rather than prolonged discussions over the telephone, Spaniards prefer, when possible, to arrange a meeting in a

Do's & Don'ts in the Workplace

Do's
- Remember that Spaniards tend to be more formal than most other Europeans, so it is advisable to err on the side of formality rather than familiarity when meeting Spaniards for the first time.
- Try to learn the appropriate greetings for different times of day and different occasions.
- Dress for the occasion. Spaniards are themselves very clothes-conscious and always dress in an appropriate fashion and you should do the same.

'ts
- not be surprised when you get kissed on both 's when you are being greeted and on both when you take your leave.
- 's are notoriously casual about keeping nts so don't expect them to be punctual.

café or a restaurant. Such meetings are usually treated as urgent and you are expected to drop everything for them. Business meetings are frequent occurrences and likely to be rather noisy affairs with everyone present seeming to talk at once and no one apparently prepared to listen. You will probably find yourself being constantly interrupted and you will need to develop determination in order to get your points across.

Because of this preference for conducting business matters over a meal, business lunches tend to become lengthy affairs. Spaniards loosen up when they find themselves in informal surroundings and much prefer to do business face to face. Most business deals and important decisions can be made over a breakfast, lunch or dinner. Generally speaking, the person doing the inviting pays the bill. 'Going Dutch' is uncommon in Spain except perhaps amongst *extranjeros* doing business with other *extranjeros*.

Office Relationships

Unlike some nationalities who do not attach much importance to building up close relationships in the office, most Spaniards much prefer to be surrounded by familiar faces. In Spain, nepotism is not frowned upon because it is common practice for Spaniards to favour family members or close friends in their business dealings. The family is a pillar of Spanish society and loyalty to one's family is undoubted. Therefore many Spaniards feel more secure employing close relatives and friends rather than comparative strangers.

The atmosphere in most offices is likely to be quite easy going and friendly. Handshakes and back-slapping among men is common and the accepted norm.

Women in the Office

Career women were rare in days gone by and were not taken seriously. Nowadays they a quite naturally in many fields which were c previously, and they are usually treated wit' and respect.

However, if you happen to want a job in a field normally restricted to men, such as selling office equipment combined with improving office efficiency, you might be greeted by raised eyebrows and an obvious lack of enthusiasm. This attitude will change rapidly if you impress the client with your speed, efficiency and confidence.

Remember the Spanish passion for kissing. You may find yourself receiving kisses on both cheeks from a businessman whom you have never met before. Don't be offended. Even if you weren't kissed on arrival, you can be sure you will be when you leave, and although you, as a foreigner, may well prefer the more usual business-like handshake, you will soon learn to accept the Spanish kisses for what they are intended... friendly greetings and farewells, nothing more!

Also, you may take time to adjust to the Spanish *tortura de la galanteria* and become embarrassed when loud comments are passed about your appearance as you walk by. This is never intended to be taken as anything but complimentary. It is not intended to be 'sexual harassment' and you would be well advised to follow the example of Spanish women who have developed the knack of acknowledging the 'compliment' in an impersonal way.

What to Wear?

Spaniards, particularly in the cities, are fashion-conscious and like to keep up with the latest trends. They will spend a good portion of their earnings on their clothes and will invariably appear well turned out during office hours. This is usually true for both men and women. The men nowadays may not necessarily stick to conservative dark- or grey suits, but even if they prefer a less 'formal' appearance, you can be sure the jacket will be extremely and smart. As for women, smart suits are probably most popular. Only in the tourist or coastal areas total informality in office-wear. However, the enquiries about local customs before appear in your office in clothes which may be able.

BUSINESS DEALINGS WITH SPANIARDS

Most foreigners say that they find doing business with Spaniards 'straightforward' generally speaking. The 'problems' (if any) seem to arise from the Spaniard's wish to enjoy what he happens to be doing at any particular moment with the frequent result that he will completely forget an appointment made a few days ago in order to pursue the business being discussed with the client sitting in front of him.

Dealing with 'Unpunctuality'

One of the chief complaints voiced by many foreigners is 'unpunctuality'. As this aspect of Spanish existence is much in evidence in all spheres, you will need to learn how to deal with:

- sudden changes of plan;
- being stood up with no excuses whatsoever offered;
- business meetings dragging on with the result that you too will be late for your next appointment.

WORKING HOURS

The rhythm of work in Spain is very different from what northern Europeans may be used to. Normal office hours are from 9:00 am to 1:00 pm or 2:00 pm, and 5:00 pm to 7:30 pm or 8:00 pm, except for banks and post offices which do not operate in the afternoon.

One young Englishman we know, setting up an office in Barcelona, employed a young Spanish girl as his secretary. He was surprised to find that although she arrived promptly each morning at 8:00 am, she would go out half an ho~ later without asking permission, and resume working~ her return without offering any excuse for her absence a couple of days, he asked her for an explanation. have my breakfast, of course!" was the surprised ~ 'breakfast-break' is common practice not only workers but also among labourers and techni~

'Coffee-breaks' (strictly timed and restrict~ countries) are non-existent in Spain. Sho~ your office to meet a business associate two or three times a day, the time spent thus will be included in 'normal office hours' and no one will think your behaviour in the least unusual.

Builders, carpenters and the like may work from 7:30 am or 8:00 am, go for breakfast at 9:00 am and then take two hours off between 1:00 pm and 3:00 pm. However, they will then continue to work until light fails.

You will be expected to adopt these hours if you work in Spain. As far as 'international business' is concerned, for instance with North America, these hours could prove to be an advantage if you take into consideration the time differences when making long-distance phone calls.

TIME OFF FOR FIESTAS

In addition, other breaks in routine are becoming common. Time off for holidays seems to vary, for example, some businesses close down entirely for three weeks around Christmas and New Year. Others simply slow down from around the 6–8 December and officially close at midday on Christmas Eve.

Ultimately, the months when major holidays do occur are the periods of least work in Spain. At these times, many

businesses run on a skeleton staff so it's a good idea not to attempt to transact any business around these *fiestas*. Advance planning is certainly a must.

VOLUNTEER WORK

There are plenty of volunteer associations in the fields of charity, health or culture in which spouses can get involved, depending on what skills they may have to contribute to such associations. It is worth contacting the relevant organisation directly to find out what is required.

FAST FACTS
ABOUT SPAIN

CHAPTER 10

'Get your facts first and then you
distort them as much as you please.'
—Mark Twain

Official Name
Kingdom of Spain

Population
40,280,780 (July 2004 est.)

Area
total: 504,782 sq km (194,897.4 sq miles)
land: 499,542 sq km (192,874.3 sq miles)
water: 5,240 sq km (2,023.2 sq miles)

Capital
Madrid

Climate
Temperate; clear, hot summers inland, more moderate and cloudy along coast; cloudy, cold winters inland, partly cloudy and cool along coast.

Currency
The euro replaced the Spanish peseta in 2002 at the rate of 166.386 pesetas per euro. One euro is made 100 cents. Coins available are one, two, five, ten, 20, and one, two euros. Notes avaialable are five, te 100, 200, 500 euros.

Languages and Dialects
Castilian Spanish (74 per cent), Catalan (17 per cent), Galician (7 per cent), Basque (2 per cent)

Agricultural Products
Grain, vegetables, olives, wine grapes, sugar beets, citrus

Other Products
Beef, pork, poultry, dairy products, fish

Government System
Spain is a constitutional monarchy with a parliamentary form of government. The king serves as head of state and commander-in-chief of the armed forces. He exercises certain executive powers acting on advice of the prime minister and Council of Ministers. Royal involvement in state affairs must be approved by the Cortes.

The prime minister, or president, proposed by the king and elected by the legislature, acts as head of government directing domestic, foreign and military policies. First and second vice-presidents are proposed by the prime minister and appointed by the King.

The Council of Ministers, or Cabinet, is recommended by the prime minister and appointed by the king.

The judicial system is headed by the Supreme Court, and Tribunal Supremo includes territorial, provincial, regional and municipal courts. Each province has its own high court which tries criminal cases.

The president of the Supreme Court, appointed by the king, presides over the General Council of Judicial Power made up of 20 judges, magistrates and attorneys, who ve full judicial power independent of the executive and lative branches and are appointed by parliament and or five-year terms.

nstitutional Court, made up of 12 members appointed ng for terms of nine years, as its name implies, is ponsible for the interpretation of the constitution. power is invested in the parliamentary Cortes

Generales made up of the Congress of Deputies which has 350 members elected proportionately according to the population of each province, and the less powerful Senate, which has 208 directly elected members and 49 regional representatives from all over Spain, including the islands and the Spanish possessions in Morocco. For both, elections are held every four years.

Regional Government

Spain is made up of 50 administrative provinces, each with its own civil governor and elected local council which in turn elects mayors of cities and towns. These provinces have been incorporated into 17 autonomous regions introduced in the Constitution of 1978 in an effort to preserve and respect the characteristics of each individual region. The strong demands of Basque and Catalan separatists led to the creation of this system, which was completed by 1983 throughout all of the regions.

Certain important powers have been delegated to these regional governing bodies such as the election of regional legislatures and presidents, management of land use, public works and transportation, social and health services and the right to speak different languages and practise different cultural traditions.

Religion

Roman Catholic (94 per cent), others (6 per cent)

Time Difference

Spain is one hour ahead of GMT, and summer and winter time changes are announced in local newspapers.

Weights and Measures

Spain uses the metric system

Acronyms

- **IVA (Impuesto al Valor Agregado)** is the equiva
  English VAT.

- **NIE (Numero de Identificacion de Extranjeros)** is an Identity Number which all foreigners need before they can make any kind of transaction, including applying for residency.
- **LRAU (Ley Reguladora de la Actividad Urbanistica)**, is known as the LAND GRAB LAW, but has been abused by some developers.

Famous People

- **Antoni Gaudi** (1852–1926) was born in Reus and became the innovative leader of the Spanish Art Nouveau movement. Best known for La Sagrada Familia in Barcelona.
- **Diego Rodriguez de Silva y Velazquez** (1599–1660) born in Seville, was perhaps the greatest Spanish painter of the 17th century. Court painter to King Philip IV, his masterpiece *Las Meninas* (*The Maids of Honour*) is an example of technical perfection for future generations. His best known painting is the *Immaculate Conception*.
- **Bartolome Esteban Murillo** (1618–1682) also born in Seville, mainly devoted himself to religious subjects.
- **El Greco** (1541–1614), born in Crete, his real name was Domenikos Theotokopoulos. He settled in Toledo. Considered, with Goya and Velazquez, as representing the acme of Spanish art, he is famous for his haunting images of biblical and religious themes as well as his striking paintings of Toledo.
- **Francisco de Zurbaran** (1598–1664) born at Fuente de Cantos in Extremadura, was a major painter of the Spanish baroque style and most noted for his religious subjects.
- **Francisco Goya y Lucientes** (1746–1828) born in Fuendetodos, became court painter in the reign of Charles IV but his best work was done separate to his official duties. Known for his scenes of violence, his etchings *Los desastres de la Guerra 1810* (Disasters of the War, 1810–1814), record the horrors of the Napoleonic invasion.
- **Juan de Herrera** (1530–1597) was the principal architect of El Escorial, King Philip II's massive granite palace-monastery which contains a beautiful library with more

than 40,000 rare manuscripts and ancient books, including the diaries of St Theresa of Avila.

- **Miguel de Cervantes y Saavedra** (1547–1616) was born in Alcala Henares, east of Madrid. He became famous after authoring the immortal, *Don Quixote* which is still read worldwide today.
- **Pablo Picasso** (1881–1973) was born in Malaga. He was probably the most productive artist of his century. One of the founders of Cubism, he spent most of his life between France and Spain to escape from the fascists. *Guernica*, a huge painting depicting the horrors of the Spanish Civil War, now hangs in the Centro de Arte Reina Sofia.
- **Placido Domingo,** born in the Barrio de Salamanca section of Madrid in 1941, is one of the most popular opera singers of the 20th century.
- **Montserrat Caballe** and **Victoria de los Angeles** are both famous sopranos.
- **Pablo Casals** (1876–1973) is a famous cellist and conductor.

Famous Sporting Names

- **Andres Segovia** (1893–1987) is considered the father of the modern classical guitar movement and has influenced thousands of guitarists all over the world.
- **Arantxa Sanchez, Alberto Costa, Carlos Moya** and **Alex Corretja** are all well known names on the international tennis circuit.
- **Severiano Ballasteros** and **Sergio Garcia** are world famous Spanish golfers.
- **Juan Belmonte, Manuel Benitez, Luis Dominguin** and **Antonio Ordoñez** are acclaimed bullfighters.

Environment

Spain faces a number of environmental challenges. Big such as Madrid, Barcelona and Gerona suffer pollutio vehicle emissions and industrial waste and large agricultural land, traditionally devoted to vineya groves or fruit orchards, are being lost to urban new motorways. Coastal areas suffer pollutio sewage and effluents from the offshore production of oil and gas.

However, more and more people are developing an interest in protecting the environment and preventing urban development from encroaching on areas of natural beauty. The government is now party to a number of international agreements dealing with issues such as air pollution, biodiversity, climate change, hazardous waste and marine dumping. The use of alternative energy is also being encouraged, with solar panels and aero generators becoming an increasingly common sight all around the country.

National Parks

Because of its varied terrain, Spain has more wild and beautiful places than any other country in Europe. Large areas have been set aside in an enlightened system of ten national parks plus hundreds of hunting and natural reserves, and other protected areas. Of the ten, the three largest and most popular are the Ordesa National Park in the Pyrenees, the National Park of La Montaña de Covadonga in the Picos of Europa along the north Atlantic coast and Doñana in the far south, a stunning bird sanctuary.

Beaches

If you are expecting to find long stretches of white sand, palm trees, warm waters and few people, you will find the Spanish beaches a disappointment. They are extremely popular with Northern Europeans, particularly Germans who have no sea comparable to the Mediterranean. Beaches which are made of fine sand can be so crowded during the summer that finding a few square inches to call your own is often quite difficult. However, if you travel further from the towns, you come across quiet spots.

many places, the Tourist Board has taken care to provide facilities at frequent intervals and a system of rating liness so that visitors can avoid swimming in water nsidered polluted. There are areas specifically for those who like to go topless or swim in the re clearly indicated by sign posts.

Purchasing Property

The building boom in Spain in recent years has caused land prices to soar and although a wide selection of property (from basic flats to luxurious mansions) is available, a prospective buyer should make caveat emptor (Let the buyer beware) his motto.

It is a good idea to seek advice from a *Notario* (qualified lawyer) before finalising your *Title Deed Escritura*. Even more important is to make sure your builder has had the plans for your house approved and possesses the necessary *Building Permit Licencia de Obras* before commencing work. One Swiss lady recently spent her life-savings on the purchase of a plot and building of her dream retirement-home only to find herself completely destitute when, soon after completion, her new home was demolished by the local council because the builder hadn't acquired the necessary permit. She had simply been too trusting!

Tourism

At one time, tourism provided material advantages for property developers, shopkeepers and villagers along the coast. Jobs became available for those without any skills, and the skilled artisan found his products snapped up in no time. Today, tourism is a major source of revenue for Spain, which has become one of the top tourist destinations in Europe. Over 53 million tourists per year visit areas along the Mediterranean coast.

Places of Cultural Interest

- **Altamira Caves in Cantabria**, discovered in 1869, boast paintings of bison and other animals from the Paleolithic period.
- **Museum of Catalonian Art**, Antoni Gaudi´s Church c the Holy Family, and the Guell Park are some of t cultural treats you will find in Barcelona, Catalonia.
- **The Old Quarter in Cordoba**, Andalusia, is famo its Islamic mosque into which a Catholic cathed been incorporated. There is also a Jewish sy close by.

- **The Escorial Monastery** near Madrid is a monument to King Philip II.
- **The Roman Aqueduct** in Segovia, Castile-Leon is one of the finest still in operation.
- **The Alhambra & the Generalife,** the summer palace of Granada kings, in Granada, Andalusia is a remarkable example of Islamic architecture.
- **The Theatre-Museum in Figueras**, Catalonia, created by Salvador Dali, is a world of folly and caprice.
- **The Bullring in Rondo**, Andalusia, is supposed to be the oldest in Spain. Traditional *corridas goyescas*, fights in period costumes from the time of Goya, are held annually.
- **Roman Ruins**, including temples, a theatre and an amphitheatre in Merida Extremadura date back to the 25th century BC.

CULTURE QUIZ

SITUATION 1

For no apparent reason, your newly installed washing machine refuses to work. As it is the height of summer and you have a houseful of family and friends, you are anxious to have the situation remedied as quickly as possible. You telephone the *tecnico* (technician) and tell him your problem. He tells you he will come '*mañana*'. '*Mañana*' comes and goes but there is no sign of the *tecnico*. You ring again and are told *"Mañana... seguro"* with the same lack of result. You fee a domestic crisis building up as the laundry pile increas in size. You:

Ⓐ Telephone a third time and lose your temper?

Ⓑ Telephone again but explain as sweetly as poss' you are at your wit's end because you have a b' house, as well as numerous other house guesr

C Hop in your car and drive furiously to the *tecnico's* office in the hope of catching him there and forcing him to come back with you and solve the problem immediately?

D Try to fix the machine yourself?

E Go out and buy a new machine which is of a completely different make?

Comments

None of the above is likely to do you much good. Perhaps **A** releases some of your pent-up frustration but nothing more. **B** merely earns you more assurances of action *mañana*. As for **C**, even if you can find your way to the *tecnico's* office, the chances are that he will be out so your trip will have been a waste of time. Good luck with **D**! It would certainly be worth making the effort if you have a bit of technical knowledge and you think there's a possibility of finding and fixing the problem, but remember if you tinker with your machine whilst it is still under guarantee, the guarantee will be invalidated. **E** would solve the problem, but it is an expensive way.

This is a situation to try your patience... the *tecnico* has not been lying to you. He sincerely hopes to be able to come *mañana* and, not wanting to disappoint you, he continues to assure you that he will. Perhaps the best solution is to shrug your shoulders, sit back and wait... or go and find the nearest launderette! You could also try some hand washing.

SITUATION 2

You decide to go out for a romantic candle-lit dinner in one of the more exclusive restaurants in your area. You are having a lovely meal, accompanied by an excellent local wine, and ʾe feeling very mellow. You are looking forward to your final ʾe solo and the smooth Spanish cognac you have learned ʾppreciate. Your relaxed mood is unexpectedly shattered ʾe sound of young voices shouting and the clatter of ʾt running between the tables. No one else seems to ʾeven notice the noise. You in turn try to ignore the ʾe expecting parental discipline to descend on the ʾo are now playing a vigorous game of 'Catch' around your table. When you find you can no longer converse with your date without shouting, you:

ⓐ Stand up, thump the table and shout at the top of your voice *"Silencio, por favor!"?*

ⓑ Shout for the head waiter and complain loudly and bitterly about the noisy children showing so little consideration for other diners?

ⓒ Try to locate the children's parents and suggest that they try controlling their charming offspring?

ⓓ Shout for the bill and leave the restaurant in an obvious bad mood?

ⓔ Order another brandy?

Comments

In fact, there is little you can do to remedy this particular situation. Answer **ⓐ** will probably earn you surprised looks from other diners, although it might possibly have a slightly quietening effect on the children if you shout loudly enough. However, the effect would only be temporary. **ⓑ** may put the head waiter in the hot seat. He may not want to offend

the big party to which the children belong. **C** is worth a try but the parents could respond in a variety of ways... ignore your complaint with a smile; make their children sit and be still; or offer you a drink and suggest you join their party. **D** is acceptable only if you have finished your meal. So why not relax and enjoy another brandy? After all, this is Spain! You can always talk later.

SITUATION 3

You have an appointment with the *notario* (notary public) for 10:00 am and arrive at his office punctually. The receptionist politely acknowledges your presence and asks you to take a seat. Two hours later, you are still sitting there and each time you catch the receptionist's eye, she shrugs her shoulders. Finally, she admits that she has no idea when the *notario* will be free. All you need is a signature on a document. You:

A Tell the receptionist you cannot wait any longer and demand that she takes you to the *notario's* private office immediately?

B Decide to take matters into your own hands by brushing past the receptionist and storming into the *notario's* office.

C Beg the receptionist to do her utmost to speed things up as you have another urgent appointment for which you are already late?

D Shout at the poor girl and leave in a huff?

E Leave your document with her and say you will come back for it later?

Comments

As mentioned several times in this book, one of the first things you need to do when you come to live in Spain is adapt to the pace of living. Punctuality is not one of the nation's most developed traits; neither is sticking to appointed times. In this situation, the receptionist is clearly incapable of helping your cause. She may not be there merely for decoration's sake but probably has neither the authority nor inclination to carry out either **A** or **C**. Answer **B** might get you in to see the *notario* who might possibly provide the required signature, but you will probably be told to find another *notario* to act for you in future. ❺ therefore is possibly a better course of action but only if you are prepared to risk losing the document altogether. Perhaps the best solution of all is what the Spaniards themselves do... the women bring their knitting or the latest romantic novel to while away the waiting hours, and the men bring a pal for a game of chess!

SITUATION 4

Your husband has been posted to Spain and his company has hired a cleaning woman on your behalf. You have been told that she is reliable and hard-working but that she speaks only Spanish, a language which at present is Double Dut to you. She is due to arrive on your doorstep shortly an are wondering how you are going to make her unde what you expect of her. You:

❶ Greet her with a smile and take her round pointing and using sign language in the hop understand what you want her to do?

❷ Arm yourself with a Spanish phrase b frequently whilst you tour the house

C Ring your husband's office and request that they send someone to act as an interpreter?

D Show her where you keep your cleaning aids and let her get on with the work?

E Tell her there's been a mistake as you weren't planning on hiring anyone just yet?

Comments

Definitely not **C**. Your husband's office may have hired the cleaner on your behalf but that's as far as their involvement in your domestic affairs is likely to be tolerated. If you opt for **E** because you hope your husband's office will find you another cleaner who can speak a little English, you will not ~~be~~ popular. If you mean to do the housework yourself, you ~~are~~ depriving yourself of the opportunity of having help in ~~the house~~, giving you more time in which to explore your ~~surr~~oundings and make new friends. **D** could lead to ~~problems~~ since the cleaner couldn't possibly know what ~~is expected~~ of her... Do her duties include washing and ~~prepar~~ing simple meals for your children or merely ~~cleaning? Obvi~~ously, it would be far more satisfactory for ~~her to hav~~e her duties spelled out, and although **A** ~~would do~~ if you happen to be a talented mime artist), **❷** is clearly the only way to avoid confusion and future misunderstandings.

SITUATION 5

You have been having a lengthy lunch with a group of friends during which the wine flowed like water, the *paella* was superb and the *carajillos* too delicious to refuse. When the time comes to break up the party, you suddenly realise you are definitely 'over the limit' as far as the amount of alcohol you have consumed is concerned. You don't have far to go to reach your house and know the road well. You:

❶ Decide to take the risk and leap in your car, hoping you won't be stopped by the police?

❷ Try to remember which of your pals was drinking mineral water and ask him for a lift home?

❸ Go to the nearest police station and explain your problem, asking them for their suggestions?

❹ Walk home?

Comments

Walking home is quite a good idea provided you are in a fit state to do so. It should help clear your head! And option **❷** is fine also as long as you can locate such an abstemiou_ pal. Answer **❶** is a no-no. Drink-driving laws in Spain me_ European norms and spot checks are quite frequent. **❸** _ possibility by only if you are far from home and none of the other solutions appear to be practical. In the local press, an incident described as *muy valorada* (praise-worthy) by the police featured a man in Benidorm who asked the local police to take care of his car as he feared he was in no condition to drive it. The police looked after his vehicle until the man returned several hours later, had a breath test which proved negative and was able to drive away. The police, in fact, are very happy to be of assistance as long as the initiative comes from the driver and no offence has been committed, but care should be taken not to abuse their willingness to offer assistance. Their help should only be sought if no alternative solution presents itself.

SITUATION 6

Your next-door neighbour is a dog-lover and has a beautiful pedigree German Shepherd which is left at home all day whilst the owner goes out to work. Bored, the dog takes to paying you a visit and, after a week or so, more or less takes up residence with you even though you have refused to offer it any form of food or drink and have sternly forbidden your children to play with it. After a while, you notice that your maid and the postman are unwilling to walk up to your front door without calling you to lock up 'your dog', who by this stage has adopted your house and family as his own, only returning to his owner when the latter comes home at night. His devotion to your family causes him to 'protect' your domain and one day he attacks an intrepid travelling salesman who has dared to wander up to your door. You:

Ⓐ Disclaim all responsibility for the attack, insisting that the dog does not belong to you?

Ⓑ Offer to take the salesman to the nearest Red Cross station for assistance?

Ⓒ Offer a sum of money as compensation?

Ⓓ Go immediately to the local police station to make a *denuncia* stating that the German Shepherd does not belong to you and was trespassing on your property when the attack occurred?

❺ Tell the salesman it was all his own fault anyway as he had no business to be knocking on people's doors to try and sell something to them.

Comments

❸ is to be avoided unless you are prepared to accept responsibility for the dog's attack even though it does not belong to you. **❹** is recommended in addition to any other option as it will protect you should the salesman in turn decide to make a *denuncia* against you, which he has every right to do. The police will then decide what action to take against the owner of the dog.

DO'S AND DON'TS

DO'S

- Get used to the idea of being kissed on both cheeks when you are being greeted and when you also take your leave.
- Keep both hands clearly visible at meal times; hiding them on your lap is considered to be bad manners.
- Treat shrines, sanctuaries, churches and cathedrals with respect. Most Spaniards are deeply religious and expect you to behave correctly in their places of worship.
- Remember that most *fiestas* have a religious origin. Despite the festivities, the occasion has its more serious side, and rowdy drunkenness will not be tolerated.
- Take note that drivers in Spain are more unpredictable than elsewhere. Most Spaniards believe in the 'survival of the fittest' so be extra careful when you take your car or moped out onto the road.
- Treat crossing the streets in general with extreme caution and remember that zebra crossings do not necessarily mean that drivers will give you the right of way.
- Respect Spanish Customs regulations.
- Be sure to seek legal advice if you are planning to buy property in Spain. Relying on your estate agent or your builder's confirmation that all is in order may not in fact be sufficient.
- Remember that oleanders, which are used prolifically as road dividers and hedges, are highly poisonous. You should always wash your hands very thoroughly with soap and water after touching them.
  Report anything of a suspicious nature to the police, bearing in mind the presence of terrorist activities in arious parts of Spain.

DON'TS

- Don't be surprised when you get kissed on the cheek by people you have only met recently.
- Don't expect to be invited into a Spaniard's home. Spaniards rarely entertain foreigners or strangers in their own houses.
- Don't yawn and stretch in public. This is considered very bad manners.
- Don't help yourself to bunches of grapes from a vineyard. 'Sampling' a few is acceptable but filling a box or basket is not!
- Don't get cross, hot and bothered when stuck in a traffic jam. That can only make the jam even more unpleasant to cope with!
- Don't underestimate the Spanish sun. Too much sun, especially if mixed with alcohol, can lead to dehydration and serious health problems.
- Don't hitch a ride or offer rides to strangers.
- Don't behave in a drunken or violent way in public or you may find yourself in prison.

GLOSSARY

COMMONLY USED WORDS AND PHRASES

Hola	Hello
Adios	Goodbye
Si	Yes
No	No
Por favor	Please
Gracias	Thank you
Muchas gracias	Thank you very much
De nada	Don't mention it
Vale!	That's fine!
Buenos dias	Good morning
Buenos tardes	Good afternoon
Buenos tardes	Good evening
Buenos noches	Good night
Como dice?	What did you say?
Perdon?	Pardon?
¿Habla inglés/ francés/ alemán?	Do you speak English/ French/ German?
No comprendo/ entiendo	I don't understand
¿Qué hora es?	What time is it?
¿Qué pasa?	What's happening?
¿Dónde están...?	Where are...?
Cómo se llama usted?	What is your name?

TRANSPORT

El passaporte	Passport
Llegadas	Arrivals
Salidas	Departures
Aduana	Customs
Entrada	Entrance

Salida	Exit
El coche	Motor car
Autopista	Motorway
Alquiler de coches	Car hire
Aparcar	Parking
La izquierda	Left
La derecha	Right
Derecho	Straight ahead
Arriba y abajo	Up and down/ above and below

DAYS OF THE WEEK

Lunes	Monday
Martes	Tuesday
Miércoles	Wednesday
Jueves	Thursday
Viernes	Friday
Sábado	Saturday
Domingo	Sunday
La mañana	Morning
La tarde	Afternoon
La noche	Night
Los dias de la semana	The days of the week

AT THE BANK AND POST OFFICE

Cambiar dinero	To change money
El banco	The bank
Cajero automatico	Cash dispenser
Oficina	Office
Abierto	Open
Cerrado	Closed
Correos	Post Office
Los sellos	Stamps

Carta	Letter
Tarjeta postal	Postcard
Inglaterra	England
Francia	France
Los Estados Unidos	United States

USEFUL VOCABULARY

Teléfono	Telephone
Estanco	Tobacconist
Mujer	Woman
Hombre	Man
Aseo	Cloakroom/ restroom
Servicios de Senoras	Ladies toilet
Servicios de Caballeros	Gents toilet
Caliente	Hot
Frio	Cold
Comer	Eat
Beber	Drink
La cuenta	The bill
Leche	Milk
Azúcar	Sugar

RESOURCE GUIDE

SERVICE TELEPHONE NUMBERS

- National Police   091
- Emergency   091
  Ask for relevant information, depending on the type of emergency
- Ambulance   091
  They will direct you towards your local community ambulance service
- Fire   091
  This very much depends on where you are but 091 should be able to give you the correct telephone number to suit your requirements.

TELEPHONES

Telefonica, the national telephone company, now has a website: http://www.telefonicaonline.com (in Spanish) which provides a wealth of detailed information for subscribers.

Some foreigners are taken aback when they pick up the phone and *"Digame!"* or *"Oiga!"* is barked at them. Either of these words is used in place of the English "Hello". Literally the first means "Tell me!" and the second *"Listen!"*, which is perfectly logical. The answerer will say *"Digame!"* and the caller will preface what he wants to say with *"Oiga!"*

Local Calls

Public telephones and telephone kiosks are available and easy to use. The rates change from year to year and need to be checked locally. Card-operating machines are becoming much more common. A *tarjeta telefonica* (phonecard) can be bought from news stands and/or tobacconists.

International Calls

You can dial directly to most countries. Since December 2000 the international code has been 00, followed by the count code (34), the area code and number. Rather than using a or hotel telephone, a simpler and more economical met of making a long distance call is to go to the local telephone office and ask the operator to place it for you. You will be sent to a cubicle when the call is connected and charged according to the meter. Many international operators are multilingual, so if you need assistance with your connection, ask for an operator who speaks your language.

'Call Back' Calls

American and UK providers of telephone services are bringing cheaper calls to Spain with 'call back' services. Using Telefonica lines, you call a unique US or UK number connected to a computer which then calls you back at your registered number with a 'cheap' line. Payments for these calls are made via credit card companies, with most providers wanting advance payment for the amount of calls you intend to make each month.

Internet

Internet facilities are now available in some specialist cafeterias. An ADSL line from Telefonica costs approximately 39 euros a month at present.

Information Resources

The British Embassy in Madrid or your local English, in some cases French or German, newspaper are excellent sources of information about the following:

- **Hospitals**—most places have their local hospitals and the larger cities can usually provide clinics which specialise in various ailments.
- **Schools and Language Schools**—as there is an ever-increasing demand for multilingual workers in practically every sphere, language schools have flourished in many areas. In some places, regional governments provide language tuition for adults. Courses for foreigners are usually four months long.
  Expat clubs, religious institutions and volunteer organisations—these can be a good way to make new friends and meet people.

Government Tourist Offices

The following Spanish government offices will be able to supply you with information on all aspects of travel and living in Spain, and their websites are usually available in both English and Spanish.

London

22-23 Manchester Square, W1M 5AP, England
Tel: (44-20) 7486-8077; fax: (44-20) 7486-8034
Website: http://www.tourspain.co.uk

New York

666 Fifth Avenue, 35th Floor, NY 10103, USA
Tel: (1-212) 265-8822; fax: (1-212) 265-8864
Website: http://www.okspain.org
Email: nyork@tourspain.es

Chicago

Water Tower Place, 845 N. Michigan Avenue, Suite 915, IL 60611, USA
Tel: (1-312) 642-1992; fax: (1-312) 642-9817
Email: chicago@tourspain.es

Miami

1221 Brickell Ave, Suite 1850, FL 33131, USA
Tel: (1-305) 358-1992; fax: (1-305) 358-8223
Email: miami@tourspain.es

Los Angeles, 8383 Wilshire Boulevard, Suite 960, Beverly Hills, CA 90211, USA
Tel: (1-213) 658-7188; fax: (1-213) 658-1061
Email: losangeles@tourspain.es

Geneva

40 Boulevard Helvetique, 67 rue du Rhone, Geneve 1207, Switzerland
Tel: (41-22) 731-1133; fax: (41-22) 731-1366
Email: ginebra@tourspain.es

Paris
43 Rue Decamps, 75784 Paris Cedex-16, France
Tel: (33-14) 503-8250; fax (33-14) 503-8251
Website: http://www.espagne.infotourisme.com

Customs

All enquiries regarding importation of goods which may cause enquiries to be made by Customs at the Spanish borders should be addressed to:

Direccion General de Aduanas, Guzman el Bueno 137, Madrid 28003

Sun Alliance Insurance SA, Compania Espania de Seguros, Tuset 20 24, Barcelona 08006

Embassies and Consulates

Alicante
British Consulate, Plaza Calvo Sotelo 1-2
Tel: (96) 521-6022; fax: (96) 514-0528
Email: enquiries@alicante.fco.gov.uk

Barcelona
British Consulate-General, Avenida Diagonal 477, 13°
Tel: (93) 366-6200; fax: (93) 366-6221
Email: barcelonaconsulate@ukinspain.com

American Consulate-General, Paseo Reina Elisenda de Montcada 23, 08034
Tel (93) 280-2227; fax: (93) 280-6175

Bilbao
British Consulate-General, Calle Alameda Urquijo 2-8
Tel: (94) 415-7600; fax: (94) 416-7632
Email: bilbaoconsulate@ukinspain.com

American Consulate, Avenida Ejercito 11–3
el: (94) 435-8300

Las Palmas de Gran Canaria
British Consulate, Edificio Cataluna, Calle Luis Morote 6-3
Tel: (96) 826-2508 and 2658
Email: Lapal-consular@fco-gov.uk

Madrid
British Embassy, Fernando el Santo 16, 28010, Madrid
Tel: (91) 700-8200; fax: (91) 700-8272
Website: http://www.ukinspain.com

American Embassy, Calle Serrano 75, 28006, Madrid
Tel: (91) 587-2200; fax: (91) 587-2303
Website: http://www.embusa.es

Australian Embassy, Plaza Descubridor Diego de Ordas 3,
28003, Madrid
Tel: (92) 535-6699; fax: (91) 353-6692
Website: http://www.embaustralia.es

Canadian Embassy, Calle Nunez de Balboa 35,
28001, Madrid
Tel: (91) 423-3250; fax: (91) 423-3251
Website: www.canada.es.org
Email: mdrid@international.gc.ca

French Embassy, Calle de Salustiano Olozaga 9
28001, Madrid
Tel: (91) 423-8900; fax: (91) 423-8901
Website: www.ambafrance.es.org

Russian Embassy, Calle Velasquez 155, 28002, Madrid
Tel: (91) 562-2264; fax: (91) 562-9712
Email: embrues@arrakis.es

Malaga
British Consulate, Edifico Eurocom, Calle Mauricio Mc
Pareto 2-2°, 29006, Malaga
Tel: (95) 235-2300; fax: (91) 235-9211
Email: malaga@fco.gov.uk

Santander
British Consulate, Paseo Perada 27, 39004, Santander
Tel: (94) 220-0000; fax: (94) 222-2941
Email: mpineiro@nexo.es

Seville
British Consulate, Plaza Nueva 8, Seville
Tel: (95) 422-8875; fax (95) 421-0323

Vigo
British Consulate, Plaza de Compostela 23-6°, 36201, Vigo
Tel: (98) 643-7133; fax: (98) 611-2678

RECREATION
Camping
Federacion Espanola de Empresarios de Camping, Calle General Oraa 52, 28006, Madrid

Diving
Federacion Espanola de Actividades Subacuaticos, Calle Santalo 15, Barcelona

Fishing
ICONA, Avenida Gran Via de San Francisco 4, Madrid

Golf
Real Federacion Espanola de Golf, D. Luis Alverez de Bohorqves, Capitan Haya 9-5, 28020, Madrid

Sailing and Boating
Real Federacion Espanola de Vela, Luis de Salazar 12-1, 28002 Madrid; tel: (91) 519-5008

Skiing
Federacion Espanola Deportes de Invierno, Avda. de los dronos, 36-A, 28043 Madrid

FURTHER READING

A visit to most lending libraries will provide you with hundreds of titles for books about Spain. Those listed below are merely ones personally enjoyed and which were found to yield the most useful information.

GUIDE BOOKS TO LIVING IN SPAIN

404 Spanish Wines. Frank Snell. Fuengirola, Spain:Lookout Publications, 1988

Spain '91. New York: Fodor, 1990.
- A very detailed source of information about travelling all over Spain and highly recommended.

Spain 2005. Fodor's Gold Guides series. New York: Fodor, 2005

A2Z of Settling on Costa Blanca in Spain. Henry Lock.
- A handy reference for anyone interested in the Costa Blanca in particular.

Annuario El Pais.
- An annual that draws together most aspects of Spanish life. Highly recommended.

Spanish Phrasebook & Dictionary. (Collins Phrase Book and Distionaries). Trafalgar Square Publishing, 1999.
- Definitely a must read.

Cooking in Spain. Janet Mendel. Santana Books, 2005

Expatriate Tax and Investment Guide. Allied Dunbar Longman. New York: Financial Times Prentice Hall, 1989.

'Guide to Acquisition of Real Estate in Spain'
- A leaflet issued by Spanish ministries responsible for Tourism, Consumer Protection and Public Works and available in six languages.

International Property Owners News.

Living and Investing in Spain.
- A pocket guide often available in bookshops.

Living in Spain. John Reay-Smith. Robert Hale Ltd, 1990 (5th ed).

Long Stays in Spain. Peter Davey. New York: Hippocrene Books, 1991.
- A complete, practical guide to living and working in Spain.

Lookout Magazine and *Lookout* Publications.
- Spain's magazines in English and highly recommended.

The Foods and Wines of Spain. New York: Knopf, 1982 (11th ed) and
Tapas: The Little Dishes of Spain. Penelope Casas. New York: Knopf, 1985.
- These two books capture the flavour of Spanish life in essays and recipes.

GENERAL READING

A Stranger in Spain. H.V. Morton. London: Methuen Publishing Ltd, 1983.

Blood Wedding: A Play. Federico Garcia Lorca. London: Nick Hern Books, 2005.
- A disturbing book dramatising the lives of Spain's repressed women.

For Whom the Bell Tolls; *The Sun Also Rises*; *Death in the Afternoon.* All three by Ernest Hemingway. (These have been reprinted by various publishers at various times. Check with your favourite bookstore.)
- These three novels depict various aspects of Spain—the Civil War, *fiesta* in Pamplona and bullfighting.

Homage to Catalonia. George Orwell. (There are a number of different editions available so check with your favourite bookstore.)

Don Quixote. Miguel De Cervantes. (There are a number of different editions available so check with your favourite bookstore.)

Iberia. James Michener. Fawcett. (There are a number of different editions available so check with your favourite bookstore.)
- A very thorough and amusing description of travels and reflections.

In Spain. Ted Walker. London: Secker and Warburg, 1987.

Spain. Jan Morris. New York: Simon & Schuster, 1988.

Spain. Sacheverell Sitwell. New York: Hastings House, 1975.
- A little dated but still a wonderful read.

The Spanish Labyrinth: An Account of the Social and Political Background of the Spanish Civil War (Canto). Gerald Brenan. Cambridge University Press, 1990.

Tales of the Alhambra / Cuentos de la Alhambra. Washington Irving, Anglo-Didacto, 2003.

The Beehive; The Family of Pascal Duarte. Both titles by Camilio Jose Cela. (Check with your favourite bookstore for the latest editions.)
- Realistic novels by the 1989 Nobel prize winner for literature.

The Spanish Temper. V.S. Pritchett. London: Vintage/ Ebury, 1975.

Two Middle-Aged Ladies in Andalusia. Penelope Chetwode, John Murray. New Ed edition, 2002.
- A very amusing account of adventures on horseback (th second middle-aged lady being the mare La Marquesa

HISTORICAL

The Spanish Civil War. Revised Edition. Hugh Thomas, Modern Library. Rev & Updated edition, 2001.

Spain: A Brief History. Pierre Vilar. Pergamon Pr, 2nd edition, 1977.

The New Spaniards (Penguin Politics and Current Affairs) John Hooper. Penguin (Non-Classics), 2nd edition 1995.
- A must for those interested in discovering how Spaniards have changed since King Juan Carlos was crowned.

ABOUT THE AUTHOR

Born in Singapore of a Belgian father and Russian mother, Marie Louise Graff is well placed to talk about culture shock. Now a British citizen, she spent her school-going years in various parts of the world including China, Malaysia, New Zealand, Australia and the USA. She has travelled extensively and speaks English, French, some basic Spanish and a little Russian.

She moved from Singapore to Spain in 1973 upon her husband's retirement. She is a member of a number of clubs and enjoys exploring Spain by car and driving around Europe with her family.

INDEX

Titles in the CultureShock! series:

Argentina	France	Russia
Australia	Germany	San Francisco
Austria	Hawaii	Saudi Arabia
Bahrain	Hong Kong	Scotland
Beijing	Hungary	Shanghai
Belgium	India	Singapore
Bolivia	Ireland	South Africa
Borneo	Italy	Spain
Brazil	Jakarta	Sri Lanka
Britain	Japan	Sweden
Bulgaria	Korea	Switzerland
Cambodia	Laos	Syria
Canada	London	Taiwan
Chicago	Malaysia	Thailand
Chile	Mauritius	Tokyo
China	Morocco	Turkey
Costa Rica	Munich	United Arab
Cuba	Myanmar	Emirates
Czech Republic	Netherlands	USA
Denmark	New Zealand	Vancouver
Ecuador	Paris	Venezuela
Egypt	Philippines	
Finland	Portugal	

For more information about any of these titles, please contact any of our Marshall Cavendish offices around the world (listed on page ii) or visit our website at:

www.marshallcavendish.com/genref